Heaven Isn't On Schedule

Elder Care For Mere Mortals

Joel Dubin

About the Author

Joel Dubin is a retired cybersecurity consultant turned humor author. This book, *Heaven Isn't On Schedule*, has some humor here and there but is about a serious subject – elder care. It's a how-to guide with vignettes about seven elderly family members he and his wife have cared for.

His most recent book, *The Norman and Phyllis Show*, is a memoir about his eccentric parents, the source of his sense of humor and his frequent inappropriate comments in public and at work.

His prior book, *The 7 Habits of Highly Dysfunctional Companies*, is based on decades of consulting work for screwed up companies around the world. He survived the corporate world with his sanity intact, though that is still debatable.

His first humor book, *Yes Dear! A Husband's Guide to Marriage*, is based on his experience being happily married for over thirty years and the lesson he learned: your wife is always right.

He speaks several foreign languages, including fluent gibberish and is a graduate of Columbia's journalism school and Northwestern's MBA program. He and his wife, Sara Guralnick, a jewelry designer and children's book author, live in Chicago.

Acknowledgements

This book is dedicated to the memory of the seven family members who lovingly cared for me and my wife when we were children, and who, in return, we lovingly cared for in their old age when we became adults.

. . . And, of course, as always, to my dear wife, Sara Guralnick, who inspires and supports all my creative endeavors with her love and compassion.

Table of Contents

Introduction

Someday, everybody will have to face it – an elderly parent or aging family member needing help. It happens suddenly, when least expected. It's never the right time, never when convenient for us. But then, it never is.

The signs were all there, staring us in the face – physical decline, memory lapses, a near miss when driving, a call from a neighbor about a fall – but we ignored them. We couldn't, or didn't, want to see them. We weren't ready.

In fact, we were never ready.

Or, maybe, deep down, we just don't want to be ready. It's not fun watching our parents get old. It reminds us of our own aging and mortality. We don't want to see it. To us, our parents are a mirror of our own elderly future, an inevitable future we don't want to face.

We once looked up to our parents. We thought they would always be there for us. We thought they would always be strong, even invincible. Then, one day, they weren't so strong.

The parents we love, vigorous when we were growing up, aren't so vigorous anymore. Basic chores have become monumental tasks. They were once self-sufficient, now they're needy and helpless. The roles of parent and child have reversed. Our parents have turned into our children, and we the children have become the parents to our parents.

It's hard to imagine being parents to our parents. You could be 70 years old, when your parents are in their 90s and, yet, they still think of you as their little baby.

It's even harder being both parents to our parents and parents to our children at the same time, especially if you started having kids when your parents have already started to age and decline.

But when the reality of aging hits our parents, it can be overwhelming. The questions start swirling around in our head. How do we take care of them? How do we manage their daily affairs and pay their bills? Can they stay at home, or will they have to go to a nursing home? How do we find a nursing home? How do we find a caregiver? How do we pay for it all?

Where do we start?

This book will help you answer those questions.

Who are we?

My wife, Sara, and I aren't health care professionals. We're not doctors or nurses and don't have degrees in gerontology. We're not social workers or therapists. We've never worked in a nursing home or as a caregiver, and we're not lawyers, financial planners or funeral directors, either.

We learned everything from personal experience in the trenches of elder care warfare.

We've dealt with dementia and belligerent behavior to setting up powers of attorney and wills, to hiring and firing caregivers and putting parents, grandparents, and other family members, in nursing homes and, finally, to arranging their funerals. We've been through the whole lifecycle of elder care.

My wife and I have had to care for and, ultimately bury, elderly family members all our lives. We've gone through this grim ritual seven times. We went through basic training helping our parents, before they succumbed to old age themselves, take care of their parents and an aunt.

By the time our four parents all needed care, we were battle-hardened and ready. But, unlike our parents, who had years to recover, emotionally and physically, between caring for their family members, we only had a little over a decade to care for all four parents. It was literally one after the other. Back-to-back elder care. No break.

It all started the summer my father and Sara's mother died three weeks apart to the day. Between shuttling between hospitals, emergency rooms and rehab for two elderly people at once, and then hastily arranging their funerals, it was a crazy summer. On top of that, my mother was already using a walker and starting to get dementia and couldn't help my father. His care fell completely on me and Sara.

That summer was so crazy that anytime someone called me, who I hadn't talked to in a while, I'd scream into the phone, "Who died?" I just assumed the worst whenever somebody called.

Once my father was gone, my mother steadily declined until we had to move her to a nursing home a few years later. Sara's father was independent, but only briefly. He eventually had a stroke and needed a cane or walker to get around. He couldn't go up the three flights of stairs of their townhouse anymore and probably should have already gone right into a nursing home.

But his mind was intact, and he insisted on staying in the house, where he had lived over fifty years with his wife and the family he raised, which included my wife and her brother. Understandably, he wanted to stay in familiar surroundings with his vast collection, gathered over a lifetime, of books and engineering tools.

We relented and let him stay in the house on one condition – he have a full-time caregiver to get groceries and cook and clean for him. We had already installed a stair lift for Eleanor when her walking started to fail. After she died, we kept them so he could go upstairs and to his bedroom.

He became incapacitated and wheel chair bound when he caught Covid. After a brief hospital stay and a stint in rehab, we had to move him, against his will, to a nursing home.

Meanwhile, we had to make sure the financial affairs for all four parents were in order. Before dementia eclipsed their minds, we had to find all their bank accounts and sources of income. We made sure powers of attorney and wills were all in order. My father, an accountant who specialized in estate planning, was completely prepared. He had powers of attorney, wills, and lists of bank accounts and contact names already all neatly assembled. He was ready.

Sara's parents, professors who couldn't be bothered with such trivial earthly matters, on the other hand, were a different story. They hired an attorney to start drafting everything, then suddenly stopped midway through the process. They never finished. They couldn't deal with it. They couldn't face their own mortality.

With the help of a brave attorney, we managed to get them to finally finish the powers of attorney and wills, hours before Sara's mother passed away. The attorney got to the hospital, papers in hand, just in time before her death. He said it was the first time he had ever had a client sign their will on their deathbed. He said it was a story for his estate lawyer buddies back at the office.

Hopefully, you will learn something from our experiences and mistakes and will avoid the drama of a family member signing their will on their deathbed.

Sadly, the problem is only going to get worse in the next decade as the leading edge of the Baby Boomers hits their eightieth birthday in 2026. They will be the largest population of elderly people in history. The demand for caregivers and nursing homes will exceed the supply.

The problem is also going to get worse as the costs of elder care keep going up, putting it more out of reach of middle-class families.

I discuss ways to pay for elder care in the chapter, Paying for Elder Care.

We've all seen people who decline and get frail in their seventies, and then we've seen others, a hundred years young, hopping and bopping on the dance floor as if they were decades younger, physically active and mentally alert until they fall apart only weeks before passing.

There is no magic number, or rule of thumb, when things start to fall apart. But our experience is elder problems generally set in between eighty and eighty-five years of age, exactly when the demand for elder care services, like caregivers and nursing homes, is expected to rise dramatically.

Elder care is more than just hiring caregivers and picking nursing homes. This isn't a guide to retirement, or about how to enjoy your retirement, or even about what to do in retirement. This is a guide about the time after retirement, when normal life ends, and aging begins to debilitate.

There are three pillars of elder care:

1. Legal Documents

2. Living Arrangements
3. Eternity Planning

Legal Documents

Even before someone reaches old age, they should have certain documents in place. Some of these, like the Power of Attorney (POA), is essential for handling any financial matters for your elderly family member, when they become incapacitated or mentally incompetent.

Of course, there are also the Living Will and the Do Not Resuscitate (DNR) for end-of-life instructions.

And, then, wills and trusts for transferring property and assets after death.

We will discuss each of these in detail, plus how to work with estate attorneys, who prepare these documents and why you should have them prepare everything rather than use canned documents bought off-the-shelf or downloaded from some web site.

While preparing these documents for your elderly family, you should do the same for yourself and your family. This will get the next generation ready, when the time comes, for your care.

Living Arrangements

When people think of elder care, they tend to laser focus on only finding caregivers and nursing homes or assisted living facilities. Rather than just telling you how to pick a nursing home, we will talk about the pros and cons of various living arrangements for the elderly.

We've had to hire – and fire – enough caregivers, and toured enough nursing homes, to give you some tips and pitfalls to avoid. Then there is also just taking care of elderly family at home. We will discuss the benefits – and difficulties – of this, as well.

Eternity Planning

This is the morbid part. Nobody likes to talk about funerals and death, and nobody likes going to a funeral home. We recommend planning funerals ahead of time, and we will discuss "pre-need," as funeral directors call it, to make this process less painful. It saves hours of hassles arranging a funeral when someone dies – when you're least prepared emotionally to handle it.

Of course, no amount of planning can ease the pain of the death of an elderly loved one. Even if you think you're ready, you're not. Even if you knew their passing was imminent, because of a terminal illness, for example, it's always still a shock when it finally happens.

A pre-planned funeral only eases the logistics, not the suffering. It's still never easy. We've gone through this seven times, as well, and will talk about our feelings and how we coped.

How to Use This Book

This book is arranged as a series of vignettes about the seven elderly family members we've cared for. After each chapter, we talk about a topic related to each family member. We talk about family issues we've experienced, dealing with difficult caregivers and nursing homes, working with attorneys on POAs and wills, handling finances and, finally, funeral arrangements.

The cast of family characters in these vignettes in order of appearance are the following:

Grandpa Al – Sara's grandfather/Eleanor's father
Aunt Pearl – My mother Phyllis's aunt
Grandma Ida – My grandmother/Norman's mother
Norman – My father/Phyllis's husband
Eleanor – Sara's mother/Sidney's wife/Al's daughter
Phyllis – My mother/Norman's wife
Sidney – Sara's father/Eleanor's husband

Those of you who know me from my humor books, won't find this subject very funny. But there is some levity here and there and, in the chapter, Dementia Diaries, we mention crazy things we've heard from elderly people, both our family and others.

My First Elder Experience

I was first exposed to elder care at the tender age of five. I had the good fortune of knowing my great grandmother. By then, it was already too late for me to get to know her. She had declined to the point where she couldn't take care of herself and couldn't speak. She just sat there motionless on the living room couch, staring into space and drooling, her runny nose dripping non-stop. I obviously really didn't, or couldn't, have had any real relationship with her.

I tagged along with my dad as he shuttled her from nursing home to nursing home until she finally landed at a place in Edgewater, a middle-class neighborhood on the North Side of Chicago.

Nursing homes weren't happy places for a young kid. They were grim buildings with dark little rooms where old people sat quietly in beds and wheelchairs doing nothing. To me, they were waiting rooms for death.

Since then, nursing homes have improved greatly. Though still not fun places, they range from assisted living with organized activities and classes and decent meal plans to fully-equipped nursing facilities providing care and companionship.

My wife and I never had children. We still didn't get off the hook for family care. Sometimes I think our mission, instead, was to take care of our family, not when they were born or in their prime, but near the end of their lives, when they were elderly. We never had to change diapers for babies but had to for our elderly parents.

This book deals with a lot of unpleasant things we never like to talk or think about: aging, illness and disabilities, nursing homes, dementia and, to top it off, funerals.

You may also resent, at times, taking care of your elderly family. It's normal. It can be a burden. You may feel you're throwing away time and money and money on someone who will be gone. With children, at least, you're investing in their future.

With children, you're paying for diapers for someone who will eventually grow out of them. With your elders, you're paying for diapers for someone who will always need them.

We say: Be obsessed with life but plan for the inevitable. Take what you learn here, put it in a drawer, and live your life. It will be there when you need it either for mom and dad or for when your kids need it for you.

We're going to start with our experience with Sara's Grandpa Al and some family issues that came up during his care.

Grandpa Al

The calls started coming every day. Your Grandpa Al has fallen out of bed again. The assisted living facility only called Sara weekly, if even that often, and then just to say he was fine. Now they were calling every day.

They didn't have the staff at night to help him up tonight. We had to go up there. They only did assisted living, they told us, and weren't equipped to help people get around, or pick them up every time they had fallen.

Assisted living was for people who could take care of themselves, do light cleaning or cooking, or at least, make their way to the dining room, if they couldn't cook.

Grandpa Al lived in a facility in Skokie, a suburb just north of Chicago. Sara and I lived, at the time, in Hyde Park, a neighborhood on the South Side of Chicago. We both worked full-time and could only go up there at night, when it was an hour drive or more because of traffic.

Grandpa Al's daughter and Sara's mother, Eleanor, put him in the facility, when he was still mobile and able to take care of himself. He had a comfortable and clean room with its own bathroom in a shared area with a refrigerator in a kitchenette.

I used to say Grandpa Al was a wedding refugee. He was living in Philadelphia, where his daughter Eleanor was born and grew up, until she married Sidney and moved to Chicago for his work. Grandpa Al had been in assisted living in Philadelphia and was mobile enough to make the trip to Chicago for our wedding, but wasn't well enough to make the trip back.

So, Eleanor kept him in Chicago and put him in assisted living in Skokie.

Everything was fine until Eleanor went away.

Eleanor Heads to Europe

Eleanor was an internationally known archaeologist, a specialist in ancient Greek and Roman artifacts. She was a celebrity at museums and universities around Europe, where she went every year to give lectures and present papers at conferences. If she happened to be in some town in Europe and just stopped unannounced at a museum or university, they would roll out the red carpet. All the museum big shots knew her.

Eleanor got her doctorate in archaeology at the University of Chicago, while her husband Sid was a professor and department chair at the Illinois Institute of Technology (IIT) close to them in Hyde Park, all while raising two kids, one of whom was Sara, and cooking and maintaining a household.

She would usually be gone every summer for at least a month, sometimes a little more.

Eleanor went off to Europe for her work, as usual, and Grandpa Al seemed fine, at least, when she left. Then, as soon as she took off, he started falling. We were the backup. The assisted living staff had Sara's number.

Sara and I Take Over

When Sara and I ran up there this time, we found Grandpa Al on the floor. He had pooped on himself. He tried to get to the bathroom, but didn't quite make it. I had to wipe him off, then carry him and put him on the toilet seat, so he could finish his business. I finally had to put some clothes on him and get him into bed.

It was ghastly.

Then, Sara and I discovered a pile of signed checks on his dresser. We noticed a bunch were missing. Eleanor had left signed checks for the caregiver to pay herself and get groceries every week. It turned out, the caregiver was more than paying herself and getting groceries. She was also helping herself to Eleanor's checking account.

Eleanor told us later she left the checks to make it convenient for the caregiver to get paid. It did make it more convenient for the caregiver – to steal. Eleanor mistakenly thought she could trust the caregiver.

While Eleanor was still somewhere in Europe, Sara and I had to step in. We took the caregiver's hand out of the cookie jar and fired her. As soon as Eleanor returned from Europe, we arranged for Grandpa Al to move to rehab. He couldn't walk anymore because his Parkinson's had gotten worse.

From then on, we helped Eleanor take care of her father. It became a shared responsibility.

The rehab at Northwestern hospital in Chicago was outstanding. They had Grandpa Al doing exercises every day. We visited him every weekend. One day, he proudly walked around the hallway normally, holding the cane in his hand rather than using it to prop himself up. He smiled as he walked by us unaided.

His freedom of movement was short lived. He declined rapidly and soon relapsed. He was wheelchair-bound again, unable to walk at all.

Grandpa Al Moves to a Nursing Home

Eleanor and Sara put him in a Jewish nursing home in Rogers Park, a neighborhood on the North Side of Chicago. At first, we were still able to get him into the car on weekends to bring him to a Jewish deli in nearby Skokie. He loved eating his native cuisine.

When it became too difficult to maneuver him into the car, we started bringing deli food to the nursing home. Soon, he couldn't feed himself anymore, and we had to help him with his knife and fork. We cut everything up into little pieces and spoon fed him.

Grandpa Al was a sweet guy. He never raised his voice and never complained. He never lost his temper or got flustered, even when we had to pick him up and clean him off. He took everything in stride. He was just happy with our little gift boxes from the deli.

Everybody at the nursing home liked Grandpa Al. He was a nice guy. He easily made friends with both the staff and residents.

Sara and I kept visiting him every weekend until he quietly passed in the nursing home a few years later.

Grandpa Al's care brought up some family issues, our next topic of discussion.

Family

Grandpa Al needed help from more than just his daughter Eleanor. It was inevitable. Elder care is always a family affair. It can bring out the best – and the worst – in family relations. Family problems, especially between siblings, stuffed since childhood, resurge with a vengeance at the worst possible time, during an elder crisis.

We once heard someone say to their sibling, "Mom always loved you best," when their elderly mother fell ill. They argued constantly and refused to help each other, and the elderly mother, of course, suffered the consequences of their neglect.

Even in the most dysfunctional families, and we've seen plenty, family differences can be overcome to provide the care needed for their elderly. We will provide some tips from situations we've observed.

We've noticed five common patterns in how families care for their elderly:

1. The Only Child
2. One Child Does Everything
3. Battling Siblings
4. Everybody Working Together
5. No Children or Runaway Children

The Only Child

I'm an only child. Everybody pitied me. Everybody said the whole burden for caring for my parents would be on me. Well, yes and no. They were only partially correct.

Sure, it was a lot of work caring for my parents, but I had help. First, my wife, Sara, gave me more than emotional support. She also helped with all the errands and chores for my parents. In turn, when she had to care for her parents, I was there one hundred percent. I more than paid her back for the help she gave me.

Second, I could make all the important decisions without consulting siblings. I didn't have to argue about whether to hire a caregiver or put my parents in nursing homes, for example, sometimes a contentious issue between siblings, or argue about what to do in an emergency. I could act on my own.

There also weren't messy legal issues or questions about dividing up estates and property. I was the only person with power of attorney and the only executor of the estate. All the legal and financial paperwork were clear and simple. I was always the sole point of contact. If something came up, all roads led to me.

It can be a lot of work taking care of elderly parents yourself. Unless you live with them, you will need help. You have no choice. And, even if you're living with them, you still need to cook and clean, do laundry, and get groceries and run other errands. Then there is picking up their medication at the pharmacy and taking them to doctors. What if you have to hold down a job and take care of your own family and kids at the same time? It's endless.

If you're not living with them, it can be a burden making sure they're being taken care of, whether at home or at a nursing home. Hiring and firing caregivers or shopping for the right nursing home is never fun.

Ultimately, only child or not, somebody has to take care of mom and dad. The question is who does what in the family.

One Child Does Everything

If you have siblings, you might think it would be easier to take care of your elderly parents. Wouldn't the responsibilities just be divided? Every family member just pulls their own weight? If only that were the case.

A common situation we've seen is where everything falls – or sometimes gets dumped – on one child. Having brothers and sisters doesn't matter. To the child carrying the load, it can feel like being an only child.

This can happen for many reasons, not just due to family problems.

In some families, one child was always the family leader. This was the kid who was always in charge. Everybody in the family might get along, but one child was always responsible for everything and was always who the family looked up to. This isn't necessarily a bad scenario. Even in a happy healthy family, one kid might have been raised, or took it on themselves, to be the family manager. It might be just how things happened. It's usually, but not always, the eldest kid.

Another common scenario is where only one child lives near the parents. In today's chaotic work world, where it can be hard to find a job nearby, or because they've been relocated by their company, kids may end up in a faraway city. Hopefully, at least one child still lives nearby. If not, someone in the family may have to come back home or, at least, plan on visiting regularly.

We ran across an interesting scenario where the responsible sibling, the big sister, lived in another city and her irresponsible brother and sister lived near mom. The big sis was constantly calling her little brother and sister to run over and take care of this or that for mom. Eventually she had to make regular visits, until mom passed, to make sure mom was being taken care of.

In this scenario, at least the kids all got along. The issue was the little brother and sister didn't know what to do. They just needed guidance.

This leads into the worst scenario – battling siblings.

Battling Siblings

All too often, families are dysfunctional. The psychological reasons are way beyond the scope of this book. Suffice it to say, these families fight on many levels. It could parent against parent, parent against child, or child against child. It could be unhappily married parents dumping on their kids. It could be kids pitted against each other by immature parents. It could be children with different personalities who just don't get along. It could be other family problems, such as substance abuse, infidelity, battered spouses, money problems, or mental illness.

We've heard a lot of horror stories. We knew of a brother and sister, who never got along, where the brother with no visible means of support took over mom's house and let it run down and then got defensive and nasty whenever the sister tried to come by. He wouldn't talk and wouldn't provide any information. He had effectively barricaded himself in the house with mom.

Any will, or power of attorney, of course, had never been settled or even put in place. It's not even clear who is in control, the elderly and sick mother, or the deranged son. When he needed money or help taking mom to the doctor, suddenly he popped out of the dark.

We know of another case, where the father was eccentric. He was a pack rat, maybe even a border line hoarder, who wouldn't discuss his finances or any estate planning with any of the kids. The children were left to fight it out and fend for themselves.

Sometimes these family problems are unresolvable. They stem from issues between the parents even before the kids were born. Then when the kids came on the scene, the problems got worse.

When something finally, and inevitably, happens to the parents, the kids are left scrambling.

These, of course, are worst case scenarios.

Then, there are families where the children get along but just disagree on what to do. Should we put dad in a nursing home or hire a caregiver?

Should we sell the house to pay for their care? Who will get the car, or other personal possessions? Who will do what to care for mom?

Difficult as it may be, someone in the family will have to take charge. If it involves getting a lawyer and going to court, then get a lawyer and go to court. It's better to try to get everything done before mom or dad passes, otherwise all kinds of skeletons could come out of unknown closets to haunt the children for years.

> *Ultimately, whatever the situation, at least one person in the family, has to take charge. The consequences could be disastrous, otherwise.*

Everybody Working Together

Yes, it does happen. Yes, there are families where everybody pulls together. Yes, there are happy families where everybody gets along. It's not as rare as it seems.

This is the ideal situation. The kids divide up the responsibilities themselves. One kid pays the bills and handles finances. Another takes care of the house. Another handles all the medical appointments. And, then, wonder of wonders, they all communicate to each other about what they're all doing. They may even have regular meetings. Fancy that!

Of course, the children have also helped the parents get their power of attorney and wills together and maybe even pre-planned funerals.

When the time comes, the kids have everything ready. There may be disagreements here and there – that's normal – but they can be worked out.

Sara and her brother Jeremy, and me as the sidekick, fit into this category. They divided up the responsibilities for Sid's care and everything ran smoothly, even when they had to settle the estate after he died.

Sara and I took care of Sid's house, paid his bills, and looked after him at the nursing home. Jeremy took care of managing his retirement and pension accounts, worked with the estate attorney to make sure the POAs and wills were together.

Sara and I also arranged Sid's funeral ahead of time with everything ready when he passed.

When we sold the house, Sara and her brother worked together with the real estate broker and lawyer to complete the sale.

Sara worked with the broker for the house, and Jeremy, who has worked extensively with lawyers in his business, talked to the attorney.

There were some small disagreements here and there, but they were small and they talked regularly and amicably worked everything out together.

No Children or Runaway Children

Not everybody has children. Even people who have children may find their kids have abandoned them. It's not guaranteed kids will hang around. They may move to distant cities, even different countries, and forget about their parents altogether.

Couples shouldn't automatically assume their kids will take care them when they get old. Kids aren't an insurance policy for elder care.

We know of an elderly couple who had one son. After graduating school, the kid took off for Europe, built a career and family and never came back. When they needed care, he wasn't around. He wasn't available. He was too distant to help. And money? They didn't save much and their kid didn't make enough to help support them. They had to rely on other resources.

If you don't have children, you might have nieces and nephews. Hopefully, you've had a good relationship with them, and they can be surrogate kids. It's not unusual for aunts and uncles to be like parents to their nieces and nephews.

And, if the family well goes dry, there might be some trusted person who you've befriended, worked with and trusted and who, hopefully, is younger and will outlive you to take care of your affairs. Non-family members can be designated as beneficiaries in powers of attorney and wills.

If you have an interesting or colorful family history or, at least, think you do, you should start recording it, either digitally or on paper, as soon as possible.

Someone in my family did all the genealogical footwork for us, tracking down records, including ship manifests and photos from when my ancestors first came to America in the 1880s. He assembled everything into a book, like a family album, complete with lots of family stories he gathered from all of us.

Sara's parents who grew up during the Great Depression and even had an uncle who painted scenes of New York from that era had a lot of great stories. We bought Sid a voice recorder to record his stories. Unfortunately, as he got older, his hands started to tremble and he couldn't use the device. So many great stories were lost.

We're going to turn next to my Aunt Pearl, a cautionary tale about caregivers, often the first step in elder care.

Aunt Pearl

The joke in my family was to never ask Aunt Pearl, my mother Phyllis's aunt, "How are you?"

The answer could be a half hour of complaints and medical test results. In fact, sometimes it was more fun going to the doctor than listening to Aunt Pearl. She would tell you about all her medical conditions, and there were many, in minute detail. She would talk about everything from her blood pressure down to her Pap smear.

Aunt Pearl the Constant Hypochondriac

There was this doctor and that doctor. She had one in every specialty. She kept medical clinics and doctor offices in business.

Then there were her medications. She took so many, her mouth was always dry. She was constantly chomping her gums and smacking her lips. We could hear her gumming from across the room.

She had a walker for as long as I can remember, a long-forgotten hip ailment from my childhood still plaguing her into old age. She had so many complaints sometimes it seemed she was born elderly.

Aunt Pearl always made sure we all knew she had stomach problems. She talked nonstop about gas and bowel movements. We got updates every time we saw her. She claimed to have the "Greenberg Stomach," some mysterious intestinal illness inherited from her mother's side of the family. I never understood what it was, but it caused her a lot of discomfort, and was her favorite topic of discussion at every meal.

She was a chronic hypochondriac, who came from a long line of whiners and complainers, the child of Jewish immigrants who came from Russia in the early 1900s, bringing their Yiddish language with them.

Her constant *kvetching* (Yiddish for complaining) aside, she was very thoughtful and sweet, always with a loving word and a big smile when seeing me. She and her husband, Sam, who owned a large clothing store in downtown Chicago, never had kids. My parents and I and my wife were her only family. We were all her kids, so to speak, the only family she had to care for her in old age.

Sunday Dinners and Dr. Kevorkian

My parents saw her once a week and, though it was an ordeal getting her and her walker into the car, usually also took her to dinner when they visited her every Sunday.

She still drove my father Norman nuts with her constant complaining. "One more peep out of you," he once told her, "And I'm going to make an appointment with Dr. Kevorkian." Kevorkian was a famous doctor convicted in 1999 of murder for an assisted suicide.

When Aunt Pearl called about something in the house, Norman, being a good sport, would run over to her Sheridan Road condo, not far from where he lived, to give her a hand.

Norman always took care of her finances. It drove him up a wall when she would try to call the CEO of a big company to complain about her dividend check, in the days before direct deposit, when it arrived late in the mail. She would demand to speak to the CEO personally, but usually only got an executive assistant, if that. Norman wondered whether the CEOs of the Fortune 500 companies providing her means of support knew her on a first name basis or had her on a blacklist of crank callers.

Aunt Pearl's complaints weren't all imaginary. She ended up a few times at St. Joseph, a nearby hospital where her doctors were. She called the crucifix on the wall above her head "*Yosele*,"

Yiddish for Joseph or protection, her way of expressing thanks to a Catholic hospital treating a Jewish patient.

Aunt Pearl still needed a full-time caregiver. My parents couldn't do it all. They hired a young lady, recently arrived from Poland. They found her on their own without going to a caregiver agency. A friend had recommended her.

The Caregiver's Side Business

The caregiver wasn't just attractive. She was very provocative. She was petite and thin with a short skirt up to her privates exposing sexy long legs and a low-cut tight blouse exposing too much cleavage. I half-jokingly asked Aunt Pearl if I could borrow the caregiver when she was off. It turned out that wasn't a joke.

The young Polish caregiver appeared to be doing a good job of taking care of Aunt Pearl until my aunt started complaining about strange men calling the condo at all hours of the day and night.

Apparently, our cute little caregiver was running a small side business. I guess she thought my parents weren't paying her enough. She was skipping out occasionally to service men in the neighborhood.

One day, the caregiver ended up in the hospital after she was severely beaten up by a customer. Her husband (yes, incredibly, she had a husband we didn't know about), came from Poland to bring her back home. That was the end of the sexy young caregiver.

The New Caregiver

My parents replaced her with a more attentive caregiver, also Polish, who was more responsible and lavished care on my aunt and, of course, dressed appropriately. The caregiver liked me, as well, since she said I reminded her of her son, who had been killed in an auto accident.

That was Aunt Pearl's last caregiver.

A few days before she passed, she called Sara and I. She wanted to see us. It was as if she instinctively knew it would be the last time.

Aunt Pearl died, of all things, from an intestinal blockage. Maybe there was something to the Greenberg Stomach. We'll never know.

Our next topic is caregivers, finding, selecting, and hiring the right one, to avoid what happened to Aunt Pearl.

Living Arrangements I: Caregivers

Aunt Pearl's caregiver story had a happy ending after a scary start. Here are some more tips for successfully finding and working with caregivers and avoiding any horror stories.

Once an elderly family member becomes incapacitated, or can't take care of themselves any longer, they have only two options: care at home or care in a facility. Care at home means either the family takes care of them, or the family hires a caregiver. Care at a facility means moving your elderly parent to assisted living or a nursing home.

Nobody wants to leave the house they've lived in for decades. Most elderly people would rather stay in their own home, if possible. Nobody wants to move into a strange place, especially assisted living or a nursing home.

Should They Go, or Should They Stay?

Caregivers versus Nursing Homes

Most people can't take care of their elderly parents themselves. A family member would either have to move in with the parent or move the parent to their house. It might sound like the easiest and cheapest alternative, but the reality of taking care of an elderly parent at home, unless they're able to get dressed and go to the bathroom themselves, for example, can be quite different.

This is aside from whether the adult children could stand living at home again with their parents. Moving back home with your parents in middle age isn't exactly the most pleasant situation. It could be returning to unpleasant family dynamics from childhood.

This leaves a caregiver as the best option for care at home.

This chapter will cover tips for working with caregivers. Nursing homes will be discussed in the chapter, Living Arrangements II: Nursing Homes.

Caregiver or not, if your parents are staying put, the house needs to be retrofitted for elder living. This means putting up handrails in bathrooms and tubs and showers, and installing electronic stair lifts, covered under Medicare if prescribed by a physician.

You may also want to consider either a medical alert device or a small intercom system, so your parents can call for help, if they fall or get stuck somewhere in the house.

A medical alert device can be worn around the neck, like a necklace, or around the wrist, like a bracelet. If they fall, or don't feel well, your elderly family member presses a button on the device that calls a dispatcher who asks what they need. The dispatcher can call for an ambulance, for example, if necessary.

The device is basically a captive cellphone programmed to only call the service's dispatcher. Like a cellphone, there are various plans. Most are monthly so they can be cancelled at a moment's notice as soon as the elderly user passes away.

How to Find a Caregiver

There are two ways to find and hire a caregiver – by word-of-mouth or through an agency. Word-of-mouth, or a personal referral, is used for finding a private caregiver.

There are plenty of private caregivers out there who work independently and not for an agency. They often work for someone for years, then when that person passes away, they're out looking for work again.

They can be found through friends, who recommend someone they once used, or maybe even through another caregiver, who might have a friend looking for extra work. Some advertise their availability on community e-mail lists, or through postings on a local service organization's web site.

Some are immigrants whose first job in America might be taking care of your elderly loved one. If your elderly parents are immigrants, who struggle with, or never learned, English, they may feel more comfortable with a caregiver from their native country who speaks their language.

Caregivers may also come from countries where caring for their elderly is part of their culture. They may have grown up in a home where typically more than one generation of an extended family – grandparents and aunts and uncles – live together under one roof, and everybody, of all ages, is expected to take care of each other. Caregiving might not be just part of the culture but also a duty.

Private Caregivers versus Agency Caregivers

Hiring a private caregiver on your own might sound easy, but there are pitfalls to avoid.

First, you're completely on your own to pay them. You pay them directly, whether through a transfer to their bank account, if they have one, or in cold hard cash, if they don't, which happens often. Legally, they're independent contractors, not employees, so they're responsible for covering their own insurance and taxes, for example.

We've known people who just pay their caregivers cash under the table and don't keep records. This is a mistake.

Even if your caregiver only wants cash to avoid declaring anything on their taxes, you should still keep payment records and issue them a 1099 at the end of the year. It's their responsibility to file and pay their taxes. If they don't, they could get in trouble with the IRS, who then might turn around and knock on your door to ask you to verify the caregiver's income. Those checking account statements showing payments to the caregiver could be a lifesaver.

My father, who was an accountant and CPA, kept complete records for every caregiver he hired for my mother. He made sure 1099s were filed every year. After he died, the IRS contacted us once when they found an error in a 1099. It turned out to be a small typo. Fortunately, we had his paperwork with the correct information and filed it with a correction. We were able to close the case quickly without incident or penalties. The lesson is that the IRS is still out there and can still find you, even if you're paying your caregiver cash.

Make sure you and the caregiver completely agree on pay, whether a salary or hourly rate, even before the first day of work. We paid our caregivers weekly for full-time, or live-in, and daily for part-timers who might only work on a weekend, for example.

We had a situation where we had two caregivers, one for the week, and a fill-in to cover the weekend. It's not unusual. It happens, and it can work. Again, make sure you agree on pay with each caregiver from the start. If the two caregivers are friends, or happen to know each other – and, believe me, they do talk to each other – make sure everybody knows exactly how much they're getting paid to avoid any conflicts.

This isn't an issue if the fill-in is from an agency and doesn't know the weekday caregiver. In that case, the pay is negotiated with the agency, as will be discussed shortly.

We recommend a fixed weekly or daily rate. Unless your parents have a punch clock at home, agreeing on hours worked can be tricky. Payment disputes can get ugly, so they need to be taken care of up front.

We had one caregiver who was transferring part of her paycheck every week back to her family overseas. We agreed to pay her on a day in the middle of the week, rather than on Friday, the customary pay day, so her family could get the funds on time at their local bank.

You're responsible if a freelance caregiver has a complaint against you, or gets injured on the job. They can still sue you, file for workman's comp and make your life miserable. If they have health or family problems of their own, and are missing work often, you have no recourse, other than to find a replacement on your own.

It's also up to you to do a background check on any prospective caregiver. You don't have to hire a private detective. A background check could be as simple as checking for credentials online. State agencies licensing, or certifying, caregivers often have ways to verify caregivers online.

Does this person have a license, or a certificate, required for caregivers in your state? Are there any complaints on file? Does this person have a police record, or any criminal convictions?

Ask for references and call them. If they run their service as a business and advertise through a web site or social media, like Facebook, or even LinkedIn, for example, check their reviews. Public sources are better, since references could be friends who were told to give five-star reviews if someone calls them.

You don't want to let someone dangerous, or who is a convicted thief or an ax murderer, in your house, let alone caring for your elderly parents.

On the other hand, agencies do, or are supposed to do, all the checks for you. They also handle paying the caregiver, sending them 1099s for taxes and are bonded and insured. You pay the agency, not the caregiver directly, and they take care of the rest. If you don't like the caregiver, or the caregiver isn't doing the job, you just call the agency to get a replacement.

Agencies may also provide training for their caregivers to make sure they meet minimum professional standards. They may also have managers to supervise teams of their caregivers. Check if the agency provides these types of additional services. This is a plus.

We had an agency once send us, for weekends only, an obese woman from Eastern Europe. She huffed and puffed just going up the stairs and barely made it around the house. Cooking and eating – more like overeating – obviously, weren't a problem for her. But she couldn't do some of the other household chores we asked of her. We thought she would drop dead of a heart attacke in our house at any moment. We told the agency we wanted someone else, and they promptly dispatched a new caregiver the next weekend.

Finding a Reliable Caregiver Agency

Caregiving agencies range from national chains to storefronts around the corner, where you can walk in and talk to someone. If they're not in your neighborhood, you can ask friends for recommendations or even search on Google. Social service organizations, through state and local governments, for example, or religious organizations – churches, synagogues and mosques – may also be able to give referrals.

There are also several trade associations for caregivers, which have employment directories.

When hiring an agency check ratings and reviews online, on web sites and on social media, including those from the Better Business Bureau. They may reveal problems not noticeable during a cursory interview or office walk through. Agencies and their staff may need to be licensed in your state. Those licenses, and complaints against them, are public records and should be available on the web sites of the state offices licensing caregivers.

Norman's mistake with Aunt Pearl's first caregiver wasn't vetting her completely. He was more careful about checking the background of the second caregiver.

The life of a caregiver can be very tough. It can be both physically demanding and emotionally draining. Besides cooking meals for the elderly, they have to change their clothes, get them out of bed, on and off the toilet (hopefully, without falls or other mishaps), and then settle them in a chair or wheelchair and later back into bed for the night. They have to clean the house and do laundry, sometimes after cleaning up poop and piss and changing their adult diapers. It's a lot of work, and it's not fun.

After all that, a caregiver may still have to put up with screaming and verbal abuse, sometimes caused by dementia, sometimes not. Sometimes an elderly parent was abusive all their life and getting old just made it worse. Whatever the cause, it still takes its toll. Some experienced caregivers have told me they're used to it. They've been through it before, and it doesn't bother them. They seem to just suck it up. We've seen some resilient caregivers. It still isn't fun.

A caregiver can stay as long as your elderly parent hasn't declined to the point where they require skilled nursing care. Depending on your parent's condition, caregivers have been known to stay for years, until your parent either passes away or ends up at a nursing facility.

My parent's caregiver took care of them for almost a decade. The caregiver for Sara's father lasted almost five years. Our experience is instructive what can happen with caregivers who stay a long time.

My father, Norman, hired a caregiver to help with my mother, since he was still working at the office during the day. My mother, Phyllis, had trouble getting around and needed help with cooking and laundry.

The caregiver worked a regular nine-to-five day until my father died unexpectedly.

After my father passed, the caregiver told us she saw my mother on the floor two days in a row when she came in the morning.

We asked the caregiver to stay full-time, including nights and weekends. We basically asked her to live with Phyllis. She agreed, and we adjusted her weekly pay to cover the additional time. At some point, the caregiver told us, since she was basically living full-time in my parent's home, she was giving up her apartment.

A few years later, she asked if her son could move in. My mom and had met the caregiver's son several times before she got dementia and told me he was "a fine and upstanding young man." So, I agreed to that too.

Then I noticed her son was now doing a lot of the work. I also noticed the caregiver herself was starting to get old and needed help. So, we had a situation where the son was now the caregiver to both my and his mother. He was, in effect, a caregiver to his mother the caregiver.

When I started getting complaints from the condo management about the son, how he bothered neighbors by smoking in my mother's, making noise coming and going at all hours of the day and night, and other erratic behavior – the doormen thought he had a drug problem – I knew Phyllis had to go to a nursing home.

I told the caregiver that her son had to move out and let her go. I gave her a month's notice, severance pay, and time to look for a new place, before I moved my mother out to the nursing home.

After they moved out, Sara and I scoured the condo and noticed tens of thousands of dollars of missing items: jewelry, watches, furs, clothing, artwork and other personal items. We ended up having to file a big insurance claim and going to the police.

On the surface, oddly, the caregiver was honest about money to a fault. She showed me a detailed list every week of how much she spent. Usually, there was cash left over, the amount matching exactly what was on her hand-written budget on the back of an envelope. I had no reason, at first, to suspect her of theft. My father had given her a credit card before he died, and I checked her purchases every week. Everything was fine. There were no outstanding charges.

But, as soon as the caregiver moved out, I cancelled the credit card.

I don't want to say the caregiver and her son acted alone. There were a lot of people who came through Phyllis's condo while the caregiver was living there. There was a cleaning lady, workmen, neighbors and friends and family of the caregiver. It could have been anyone.

I was working and had my own family to take care of. I could only come and visit once a week for about an hour. I didn't know what was going on the rest of the week. I didn't see things disappearing.

We asked Phyllis, for example, if we could take the jewelry and furs out of the house. She yelled and wouldn't let us take anything. In her demented state, she put a few pieces of fine jewelry under the

mattress in front of the caregiver. There they sat —
the caregiver and her son knew where they were —
ripe for the picking.

At Sara's father's house, we noticed expensive
silverware, and other decorative items, missing
when we were setting the table one night. Other
expensive items Sid and Eleanor had collected from
their travels seemed to have disappeared. There
was a revolving door of people through the house,
all temporary caregivers on the weekends — for a
while it seemed like there was a new one every few
weeks. Again, as with Phyllis, there could be any
number of suspects.

When caregivers stay a long time, they get
comfortable. Sometimes they act like they own the
place. But they don't, and they need to be
supervised carefully. They may think, as your
elderly parents decline, they won't notice a few
things missing here and there.

I'm not saying, at all, that all caregivers steal. The
majority you will hire are fine and honest. You just
need to be aware of what can happen.

Some caregivers come from desperately poor
countries. In their eyes, even though you may be
of modest means, they may think you're fabulously
wealthy. Compared to them, you are. The Social
Security check you may be using to cover part of

their pay might be more than several month's pay in their home country.

Other Potential Problems with Caregivers

Make sure to remove any financial documents from the house, like bank statements, mortgage documents or statements from 401K and IRA and other investment or brokerage accounts. Nobody outside your family, including caregivers, needs to know your finances.

The only credit card at the house should be the one you may give the caregiver for groceries or other household expenses, for example. It should have a low limit, and should be checked weekly or monthly for outstanding charges.

Likewise, any valuables, such as jewelry, furs, or collectibles, for example, should also be taken out of the house. Make an inventory of everything your parents have in the house and keep it somewhere safe outside their home.

You will need to keep Internet and cellphone service on, so your parents can watch TV and keep in touch. But these should also be checked regularly, either weekly or monthly, for misuse or overseas calls, at your expense, to the caregiver's family back home. Routers for Internet service should be password protected, with remote access removed, and all access logged. These should also be checked regularly for tampering.

If the caregiver wants a streaming TV package in their native language – especially for entertainment, if they're living full-time in the house – it's up to you if you want to pay for it. Just make sure they're not putting it on your bill without your knowledge.

Again, most people have great experiences with their caregivers. Just be aware, as with any service, things can happen, and you need to protect yourself.

Paying for a Caregiver

Caregivers can range in price, depending on whether they're private or through an agency. Since rates vary both by locality and type of care, it's hard to give a ballpark estimate. But expect to pay upwards of 1,000 dollars a week or roughly 4,000 dollars a month.

That's on top of all the other expenses for upkeep for your elders, such as meals and groceries and home supplies, and utilities and electricity. Then for apartment and condo dwellers, there is rent and assessments. Hopefully, the mortgage is already paid off, leaving one less monthly expense to worry about.

Medical expenses should be covered by Medicare or Medicaid, depending on your age and income. Medicare starts at age 65, so we're assuming your elderly mom or dad is at least that old.

Since a caregiver works in your home, you can't sell the house, a possibility for paying for a nursing home. There are other sources of financing without giving up your parent's house. Start with Social Security and pensions. Your parents may be old enough to have started working when companies still gave their employees pensions.

Otherwise, depending on your parent's finances, there may be savings, 401Ks and IRAs, and assets such as stocks and bonds.

We know of two brothers who couldn't afford caregivers or nursing homes and found a creative way to take care of their mother at no cost. They arranged their work schedules so one brother could work at night and the other during the day. When one was working, the other was at home with mom.

Not everybody has that luxury, and eventually, if they live long enough, your elderly parents may require more care than any family member or caregiver can provide.

We know of one family where their mother, who had dementia, lived fine with them at home. They were able to take care of her for a few years, until she started walking around the house naked in a daze. She didn't know where she was or what she was doing. The family knew it was time to move her to a nursing home.

The story of Grandma Ida who terrorized her nursing home is next. She didn't walk around the house naked in a daze but was more than a handful for any caregiver. When she started calling us with bizarre requests at odd times and started mixing up her medications, we knew she needed nursing care.

Caregiver Checklist

- Private/independent or through agency
- Find agency via ads, search, social media
- Check agency's records with the state
  - ➤ Is the agency bonded and insured?
  - ➤ Does the agency train caregivers?
  - ➤ Does the agency supervise caregivers?
  - ➤ Check references and online reviews
- Agree on price and draft work agreement
- Issue 1099s to independent caregivers
- Agree on hours and days of week
- Remove important papers from house
- Remove valuables from house
- Visit regularly to check care, cleanliness
- Record of all expenses and credit cards

Grandma Ida

My Grandma Ida, Norman's mother, terrorized her nursing home. She lived to 100, outlived three husbands, drove herself to her ninetieth birthday party, and got a speeding ticket a few years later at the age of 94. Nothing slowed down Grandma Ida, not even the cop who stopped her.

"You can't give an old lady a ticket," Grandma Ida protested to the officer. He disagreed, and she lived to complain about it to her friends and family. Shortly afterwards, she had the good sense to sell the car and let her big family in the Minneapolis area chauffer her around.

She knew she shouldn't drive, but otherwise was totally self-sufficient, still baking boxes of her famous thimble cookies and lemon squares well into her nineties. The cookies got their name from the well, the size of a thimble, where she poked the dough and dropped in a dab of jelly.

Grandma Ida was energetic and feisty. I profile her in my previous humor book about my parents, *The Norman and Phyllis Show*.

We thought she would make it to the finish line without help. Independent and overbearing, nobody was going to tell Grandma Ida what to do.

Nobody was going to push her around, until old age arrived with other plans.

Grandma Ida lived through the Titanic, two world wars, the flu epidemic of 1918, the Great Depression, and the Korean and Vietnam wars and the social upheaval of the 1960s. She was born when movies were silent and only black and white and lived to see personal computers and the Internet.

She seemed to go from independent to dependent overnight. Shortly after turning 95, she was forgetting to take her medication. She was confused and calling us at random at odd hours with weird requests out of the dark. She went from mentally sharp to out of it.

Norman had to fly up to Minneapolis and get her on a plane and bring her back to Chicago. My dad quickly arranged to put her in a nursing home near his house in the city. She went directly from the plane to the nursing home.

Grandma Ida Takes Over the Nursing Home

The craziness started shortly after she arrived at the nursing home. Physically, she was fine. She could walk without a cane or walker and would push her wheelchair herself, rather than ride in it.

Grandma Ida didn't need no stinking wheelchair. She would show them.

And show them she did. She was still somewhat lucid at times in the beginning. Shortly after arriving, she went from room to room and told everybody, "Anybody that can see or walk, we're getting out of here." The surprised security guard at the entrance stopped Grandma Ida and her posse of over a dozen able-bodied residents as they were getting off the elevator and heading to the front door.

Later, at dinner, she stood in front of the cafeteria and thanked everybody for coming to the wedding. A few times, when my dad visited, she would lean over and ask him for cash, so she could tip the waiters. She also told him she was taking the train the next day to visit some out-of-town relatives. She asked me once why my brother — I'm an only child — never visited.

I learned from Grandma Ida to never reason with someone who had dementia. It was pointless. Just say yes and agree. They won't know the difference.

Norman was very diligent about visiting Grandma Ida at least once a week. He hired a caregiver to come in and watch her for a few hours every day. Sara and I pitched in and went to see her every weekend, often bringing her some sweets. Her sweet tooth lasted until nearly the end.

Norman sold her house in Minneapolis and took care of her finances. Grandma Ida had owned a gift shop and was very frugal. My father, who was a CPA and understood investing, made sure her savings were well taken care of. With her savings and Social Security, paying for nursing care, though expensive, was still in reach.

Gradually, her body also gave out, and my father wouldn't let me or Sara see her when she started to decline sharply near the end. She quietly passed away from old age at the nursing home.

Sara and I helped my dad every step of the way from cleaning out her house and getting rid of all her furniture and other stuff to picking the nursing home and supervising her care. We also were involved in the funeral planning.

Our next topic is nursing homes and not just about how to pick one.

Living Arrangements II: Nursing Homes

Other than Grandma Ida trying to stage an elder coup d'etat at her nursing home, and driving us all nuts along the way – my father, Sara and I and the nursing staff – her stay was uneventful. She didn't have any falls or medical emergencies and the staff competently managed her care.

Others aren't so lucky. The nursing home experience, from picking a facility and moving in to dealing with daily care, can be a nightmare. The whole process can be emotional for both you and your parents.

Even regular visits, after they're settled in, can still be heartbreaking. The pain never goes away.

Where your parents live will depend on their mental and physical state. If they're still physically and mentally active but just don't want to take care of a house or condo anymore, they may consider moving to assisted living. If they're not physically or mentally able and can't be cared for at home any longer, even by a caregiver, they will have to move out of the house, even if they don't want to.

Besides nursing homes, there are other types of long-term care facilities providing nursing services.

Your elderly parents won't care what it's called. It's still not home and doesn't feel like home. If they were forced to move because of their condition, expect resistance. Be prepared. We weren't and will provide tips on how we learned to cope.

If your elderly parent has been living alone until now, they may not be used to communal living in a facility. Some may welcome meeting new people and making friends and may love the comradery. Others who aren't so outgoing may hate the forced socializing. They may feel isolated and alone with a bunch of strangers, or worse, like they're in prison.

In this chapter, we'll explain the different types of living arrangements for the elderly, including nursing homes, and how to pick the right one for your parents, and then how to manage their stay.

They're Not All Nursing Homes:
The Different Elder Care Facilities

Not everything called a nursing home is a nursing home, and not all nursing homes are the same.

Our experience is there are three general types of facilities for the elderly.

1. Assisted living
2. Memory care
3. Skilled nursing

Let's go through each one from those for the most independent elderly needing minimal care to those for the most incapacitated requiring the most care.

Assisted Living

Assisted living offers the least care. It doesn't have to. It's designed for elderly people who can still take care of themselves and do daily activities on their own, such as putting on their clothes, bathing, eating and going to the bathroom. Some might still even be able, and eager, to cook and clean for themselves.

The idea is to provide an environment free of daily maintenance and household chores. Assisted living facilities vary in the range of services they offer depending on the needs, and conditions, of their residents. Some may offer more care and support services than others. Either way, make sure, when picking a facility, it meets the specific needs of your elderly parent.

Residents may have some mild memory issues but are aware of their surroundings and alert enough to hold an intelligent conversation. They're not likely to get up in the middle of the night and drift out of the building.

Assisting living isn't for those with serious dementia, especially if they're confused enough to miss meals or miss taking medication, or don't know where they are.

Living arrangements range from single dorm-like rooms to small furnished apartments. They may have kitchenettes for those still wanting to cook but may also have a cafeteria or other common dining area, where meals are already prepared.

They may also offer activities, like arts and crafts, discussion groups – sometimes even in foreign languages spoken by residents – a movie theater and even a library. They may offer dance and exercise classes in an exercise room with minimal equipment for light workouts. A schedule of movies and other events is usually posted on a message board on a wall.

The staff is only enough to maintain the place – administrative staff, social workers, maintenance people, and cooks – usually only working normal business hours. There aren't doctors, nurses, or other medical staff on-site.

The daily routine starts with staff going to each room every morning – a wellness check – to see if everybody made it through the night or just needs extra help. At night, the only staff are maintenance people and a receptionist at the door to make calls in case of an emergency.

If you're elderly parent slips deeper into dementia, or has difficulty moving around, maybe even confined to a wheelchair, they may need to be moved to the next level of nursing care, either memory care or skilled nursing.

Some elder care companies offer the whole range of nursing services, of which assisted living is only one part. In that case, your elderly parent in assisted living can move to the skilled nursing section, wherever it's available, either in the same or different facility in their network.

Memory Care

We have limited experience with memory care. All our elderly family moved straight from in-home caregivers to a nursing home, bypassing the memory care stage.

What we know is from what we've observed at skilled nursing facilities also offering memory care. Memory care offers some of the same care as skilled nursing except with extra services tailored specifically for dementia and Altheimer's patients.

They may appear the same bur are two entirely different types of services. Memory care usually isn't in a separate facility. It's almost always a specialized unit within a nursing home.

Check these services before considering memory care for your elderly parents.

These services should include medical staff, both doctors and nurses and their assistants, all specially trained in treating dementia patients. Doctors and practical nurses should be available on call, like at skilled nursing homes.

The building entrances and exits should be locked and any attached outdoor recreation areas should also be fenced in and locked to prevent residents from wandering off. There should be a receptionist at the front entrance 24x7 for security. The receptionist should also have access to all security cameras that should be posted around all building entrances and exits.

The next step after memory care is skilled nursing.

Skilled Nursing

Visiting a skilled care nursing home, even a nice one, can be heartbreaking even on a good day. What you see may be shocking and upsetting.

Disabled patients in wheelchairs, some wrapped in blankets, others not, some staring into space, others babbling gibberish, if not occasionally yelling, sometimes obscenities, are all common sights. Being around physical, and sometimes mental, human wreckage can be very upsetting. Sometimes you get used to it after a while, sometimes not.

Sometimes there is humor in the little dramas among residents to lighten the atmosphere.

When I visited my mother the first time after moving her to a nursing home, another resident sitting next to her in a wheelchair said to me, "We're keeping an eye out for your mother." For a minute, I thought she was part of gang at the nursing home. It turns out that woman, whose name was also Phyllis, was the day room heavy. Whenever the other Phyllis spoke up, the staff would come running.

During regular visits, Phyllis only smiled at me. I assumed she still knew who I was, even though she had forgotten my name. She would then pull me close to her and kiss me on the cheek. Another resident sitting nearby once said, "Isn't that sweet."

When visiting my mother another time, I heard someone singing, "I can't live without you," loud enough for everyone in the day room to hear. Another resident sitting nearby piped up after a while, "Shut up already!"

On the bright side, there may also be activity rooms with people playing bingo or board games, or doing some arts and crafts, if they're hands are still able. People may be sitting around tables talking, probably about "the good old days" when they were decades younger.

At the nursing home where Sara's father Sidney lived, he played bingo every weekend. He sat at a long table with several residents, all in wheelchairs. At the head of the table, another resident, physically and mentally able to spin the bingo cage, called out the numbers. Sid won a lot, and I noticed some of the ladies would wheel up next to him to be close to the bingo shark.

If Sid happened to be playing bingo when we visited, we left him alone. We had to let him play. He was too busy being the big the shot getting attention from the elderly ladies at the bingo table and couldn't be bothered.

Sid thought he was saving money from bingo for a taxi to go home. Both the winnings and the taxi were in his imagination.

Finding a Nursing Home

You can look for nursing homes the same way you would like for a caregiver, as previously discussed in the chapter, Living Arrangements I: Caregivers. You can use personal recommendations, searh online or with AI, check advertisements on TV and social media, or even just walk into a facility in your neighborhood.

There are also online directories and referral services like A Place for Mom. The large number of facilities and their services can be confusing. A referral service can help you pick out the right facility at no charge. A Place for Mom charges the only after placing your elderly family member in assisted living or a nursing home.

First Walk Through the Nursing Home

Before considering any nursing home for your elderly parents, you have to visit and do a walkthrough. Don't go by flashy ads or slick web sites. Pictures of smiling staff and residents in marketing materials and on web sites can be deceiving.

We've gone through these visits over a dozen times and can offer some tips on what to look for. Most visits follow the same pattern.

First, before even sitting down with a representative, get a general feel for the place. Are the people at the reception desk helpful? Does the entrance seem secure or, in other words, do you need to ring a bell and be buzzed in, or can anyone just walk in? If you can just walk in unannounced, your elderly parent, with dementia or just plain confused, can likewise walk out unnoticed.

You will then be escorted to a management office, or a conference room, where a representative will go over details about what the home offers, its facilities, room availability, and the most dreaded part of all, how much it will cost and how to pay for it.

After the initial meeting, you will want to see the facility. Pay close attention to the atmosphere inside, beyond just the reception area and the management office. First, the obvious. Is it clean, or does it smell of urine and poop? Do the floors look like they've been washed recently? Is it well lit, or does it look like a windowless dungeon? Does it look more like a hospital wing or, as much as possible, like someone's home?

Is there a nursing station accessible to every room, or at least on every floor? Can everyone contact a nurse immediately from their room by an intercom, usually a device with a big call button attached by a cable to a wall. If someone needs to go to the bathroom immediately and needs help getting out of bed, will someone be just a call button away?

Do the residents seem relatively calm, or is there constant chaos and confusion? Does the staff look like they're always running around in the halls, as if constantly in crisis? Do the staff have a good attitude, or do they have a chip on their shoulder? Are they annoyed, or helpful, when you ask them a question?

The walkthrough with a representative should also include recreation areas, large rooms, like day rooms, where residents sit and gather, eating areas or cafeterias and physical therapy or exercise rooms.

It's hard to dress up even the nicest of nursing homes to not look like a glorified hospital wing. But there are little things that make a difference, such as cheery artwork on the walls, photos of staff and residents at events, or displays of sample arts and crafts done by residents. Decorating for the holidays is also a nice happy touch.

Check if there are daily activities for residents. Are they just wheeled out every morning into the hall or put in a day room with a blaring TV and left alone there all day?

There should be things to do, for those who are able. Check if there is a calendar on a wall in big print with a schedule of activities. Is it full, or does it have a lot of gaps and empty spaces? Are there a lot of interesting events, that might even interest you? For example, at one nursing home we visited with a lot of elderly Jewish residents, I noticed the calendar had a regular conversation group in Yiddish, the colorful language of Sara's and my ancestors, where even I thought of dropping in to hear some interesting stories from before my time.

We've seen nursing homes equipped with arts and crafts or exercise areas. We also saw one nursing home that had concerts and singers come in occasionally to serenade residents during meals.

What are the eating arrangements? Look at all the common eating areas. Most nursing homes don't have a traditional cafeteria for residents, most of whom might not be able to stand long enough in a line at a counter.

We've observed that meals are either brought to the resident's room, or they're brought to a common dining room and served there. Does staff help residents who can't feed themselves, or are residents left to struggle on their own with knives and forks? Check if there is a menu and if there is a variety of dishes or just the same old slop every day.

It may not be on the tour, but see if there is a common shower area where residents are showered or bathed by staff. Rooms shouldn't

74

have showers or tubs for safety, which are slip hazards.

Check what medical care is on-site and how emergencies are handled. There should be 24-hour nursing staff. Doctors and practical nurses, on the other hand, may make regular visits but are only on call otherwise. Ask what are the procedures for emergencies after hours. The nursing home should call you if, for example, your parent falls and is injured or suddenly gets sick.

Our experience has been the nursing home will contact you before calling either a doctor or an ambulance. You should give the nursing home back up numbers in case of an emergency for either your spouse, another family member, or a friend. Make sure someone is always available.

When our parents were in nursing homes, we made sure one of us had our mobile phones always by our side just in case. We made ourselves available 24x7.

Ask the representative to show you a room. Most rooms are either single or double rooms. In double rooms check if there is a curtain between the beds that can be pulled around the bed for privacy. As with the rest of the facility, check if the room is clean, well-maintained and doesn't smell of urine or any other bodily secretions.

Check if the bathroom has handrails and if raised toilet seats are available. Likewise, see if the bed has guardrails to prevent your mom or dad from falling onto the floor, from either rolling out of bed or trying to get up.

If there is a refrigerator in the room, make sure it works. There should also be a closet with hangers for clothing and coats.

And, of course, make sure there is a call button, accessible and easy to use for arthritic or gnarled fingers. The call button should go directly to the closest nursing station.

How many nurses and other staff are either at the nursing station or in the halls and rooms doing chores? Does it seem like there is enough staff, or does it seem like it takes forever to get help since no one is around?

The work can be physically and emotionally exhausting. Moving and lifting residents into and out of beds and bathrooms takes strength. Changing diapers on an elderly adult two or three times a day, or more, isn't much fun either. If a resident is belligerent or combative, it only makes an already unpleasant situation more unpleasant for everybody.

We've noticed that many nursing homes lately seem to be chronically understaffed. Since Covid, when many nurses quit over long hours and heavy workloads, and just plain emotional exhaustion, nursing homes have relied on contractors for backup staff. Full-time nurses get to know the residents and build bonds and relationships. Contractors come and go for short periods of times and don't build relationships with residents.

The Byzantine Application Process

Once you've chosen the nursing home, next is the fun part – mountains of paperwork. Every time we've put an elderly family member in a nursing home, without exception, there is enough paperwork to choke a bureaucracy. An administrator or someone in the office will send you, emails with the documents on DocuSign, at least a hundred pages long to review and sign.

Nursing homes are regulated by various state and federal agencies, including Medicare and Medicaid, and need seemingly endless amounts of paperwork as evidence for inspectors and auditors, not to mention attorneys, in case of lawsuits.

Of course, they will need contact information in case of emergency. Give them more than one number, such as your spouse's, other family members, a neighbor, or some other trusted contacts. They should go down the chain of numbers, calling everyone on the list until they reach someone.

Besides the paperwork from the nursing home, they will also want medical records from your parent's most recent physician. They will also ask for a Do Not Resuscitate (DNR), which are the instructions, as the name implies, for when your parents stop breathing or appear to have passed.

We'll discuss DNRs and living wills in more detail in the chapter, Legal Documents I: Powers of Attorney, and about funeral home stuff in the chapter, Eternity Planning.

The nursing home may also ask for the name of the funeral home, where your mom or dad should be taken, when they pass. We've been amazed how quickly the nursing home cleans out the room and gets it ready for the next guest, often the same day, after our family members have passed.

The paperwork all processed, next is moving your parents to the nursing home. Depending on how mobile they are and how much stuff you've packed to bring along, you may need to hire a medical transport company. These are services with specially fitted vans with straps for carrying wheelchair-bound passengers.

You should only pack a few items, even less than for a hotel stay.

The nursing home will ask you to bring clothing and shoes but otherwise they supply everyday toiletries like soap and shampoo. It's up to you – the nursing home won't bring it up – if you want to bring family photos or other memorabilia to keep your elderly parent still feel connected to their family.

We also noticed our parents sometimes wearing clothes other than those we brought. We noticed the laundry at the nursing home washed everybody's clothes together in one big bundle and then doled them out at random to residents. As long as the clothing fit, no matter the original owner, the staff dressed residents with whatever came back from the laundry.

Some nursing homes put name tags on clothes and laundry bags. But clothing sometimes still gets mixed up.

So, other than fancy clothes there are other items your parents should never bring to a nursing home. The list includes any jewelry, even inexpensive costume jewelry, wristwatches, and cellphones. We've noticed these things tend to disappear.

You should only bring books and magazines, if your parents are still able to read. In Phyllis's case, I brought a bunch magazines she used to like to read, then saw them sitting in the same spot for weeks.

Sara's father, Sid, on the other hand, even after he stopped being able to read – he read 300 to 400-page books every week when he was younger – could still enjoy big coffee table books with pictures and artwork. He had been an engineer and particularly liked books with diagrams of the inner workings of ships and airplanes. Sometimes, he would look at them while we were talking to him when we visited.

The room should have a telephone with a direct dial number, so they shouldn't need a cellphone or have to go through a switchboard. It should be on a table within easy reach of their bed or chair. The phone should also have a volume control for both the ringer and the voice, which can be made loud enough for them to hear.

Once when we visited Sid, he asked why we never called. Sara called Sid right there from her cellphone, and the phone rang loud and clear – to us, not to Sid. We turned the volume up on both the ringer and the voice. Problem solved. No more complaints about us not calling.

The Dementia Radio

Another item we bought for Sid was a dementia radio – yes, that's exactly what it's called. Sid loved listening to classical music, even after his dementia had progressed to the point where he couldn't read anymore. But he couldn't work the radio we had given him. The buttons were too small for his shaky hands and, his weak eyes couldn't read the dial.

The dementia radio was a sturdy rectangular box with rubber footies that sat squarely on the table to keep it from falling off. It had a huge round on/off and volume switch and four large buttons, big enough for even Sid's shaky hands to use, each pre-set for a different station. Since the stations are preset, there were no dials too tiny for Sid's elderly eyes.

The settings were behind a panel screwed shut on the back. We unscrewed the back door, preset the stations, and then screw it shut again.

Before we got the dementia radio, Sid would call us and say the radio wasn't working. He said he couldn't find his favorite station. It was working, and his favorite station was there. He just couldn't use it anymore. After getting the dementia radio, he enjoyed his classical music, sometimes a bit loud, without asking us to come up and fix the radio.

Visit as Often as Possible

It's a good idea to visit your parents in the nursing home regularly. It doesn't have to be every day, but should be at least once a week. Three to four times a week is ideal, but with work and other family obligations, life often gets in the way.

The more often the nursing home staff see your face, the more attention your family member will get.

You should also schedule a meeting every few months with the management and staff to discuss any issues or complaints about the care your parent is receiving. We've found these face-to-face meetings very productive.

A nursing home isn't a place to just dump your parents and forget about them, which, unfortunately, some families do. You still need to pay attention to how the nursing home is taking care of mom or dad, just as you would with a caregiver.

You need to be the advocate for your parents at the nursing home.

Palliative Care and Hospice

One invaluable service we used for every family member in a nursing home is palliative care. Palliative care is a service that provides a second set of eyes on your parents. The service is free to you, since the companies bill Medicare directly.

The service sends a nurse dedicated to your parents to visit the nursing home anywhere from every few weeks to monthly. They will work directly with the staff to check in on the status of your parent's health and make recommendations about what medications they should be taking, or not taking. They will prune unnecessary medications from the list.

Palliative care companies also provide, when the time comes, in-house hospice services. Generally, hospice care is only for terminally ill patients. But if your elderly family member has declined substantially and isn't responding to normal care and medication, inevitable even with the best nursing care, the company will send a physician to evaluate whether your parent qualifies for hospice care.

There will be paperwork to sign to make the transition but, as with palliative care, Medicare is still billed directly.

The hospice staff will visit the nursing home more often, at least once a week, and will take charge of any emergencies. The nursing home no longer calls an ambulance to take your parent to the hospital. They call the hospice service, who will dispatch a physician to see the patient.

If you're not satisfied with the hospice service, you can switch back to palliative care. It's up to you. With hospice, the service takes over some of the care provided by the nursing home, even while they're still in the nursing home. With palliative care, the nursing home still controls your parent's care.

When the palliative care service said my mother, and later Sara's father, had declined to the point where they needed hospice care, we learned that hospice care, unlike what we had previously thought, was an extra layer of care and not just for the terminally ill.

A nice touch the hospice service provided for my mother was regular FaceTime calls. My mother went into hospice at the height of the Covid pandemic. For the last few months of her life, I couldn't go visit her. Whenever I saw the hospice nurse's number on my cellphone, I knew it was my mother calling. It made all the difference being able to see her, if even only over the phone. It made me feel like I was still at my mother's side, even if only virtually, up until the very end.

If you're unhappy with the nursing home after a while and want to make a change, keep in mind that moving your parent to another home can be painful for everyone involved. It can make your elderly parent more confused and disoriented. Unless you're ready to sue, since the care is so bad, or your parent is falling a lot from a lack of attention, mom or dad should stay put.

Our experience is that the average stay in a nursing home is only around two years. We've heard stories of people staying as long as ten years, but that's the exception. Phyllis was closer to the norm at two and a half years, and Sid was somewhere in between at five years.

Paying for A Nursing Home

The next million-dollar question – literally – is how to pay for a nursing home.

We've already discussed in the chapter, Living Arrangements I: Caregivers, about the two costs for caregivers: one for the caregiver and the other for meals and household expenses.

With a nursing home, all those expenses – salaries and room and board – are rolled into one. Make two budgets, one itemized for a caregiver and the additional household expenses, and the other, for a nursing home. The nursing home should be one single payment each month. This way you can compare the all-in costs for both options.

One way to save on a nursing home is to put your parent in a double room. Single rooms can be, not surprisingly, as much as double the cost of a double room. My mother's dementia was so far advanced she didn't even know she had roommate. She was fine with everybody assigned to her room, and we saved money with a double room. Sara's father, on the other hand, wanted his privacy and was aware enough to not want a roommate. As a result, we had to pay for a single room.

Surprisingly, for my mother, the total monthly cost of a caregiver plus household expenses was the same as the single monthly payment for the nursing home. But that isn't necessarily the case, and the nursing home could come out more expensive.

Ultimately, the same formula for paying for caregivers applies to paying for nursing homes, a mix of pensions, IRAs and 401Ks and, of course, social security and other savings. With a nursing home, since your parent is no longer living at home, you have the additional option of selling the house.

If you have to rely on Medicaid, your options are limited to facilities accepting Medicaid, which might not be conveniently located. Check with your local Medicaid office for more details.

Ideally, before your journey with caregivers and nursing homes, you should have, at a bare minimum, powers of attorney, both for property and health care, and wills in place and, if possible, pre-planned funeral arrangements.

Next, we'll talk about my father, Norman, whose business included doing estate planning for high-net-worth individuals. He did everything right. Everything was in order, except for one hitch.

Nursing Home Checklist

- Decide on the type of facility
  - ➤ Assisted living
  - ➤ Memory care
  - ➤ Skilled nursing
- Visit the facility
  - ➤ Meet management
  - ➤ Cleanliness
  - ➤ Adequate staffing
  - ➤ General atmosphere
  - ➤ Location of nursing stations
  - ➤ Availability of doctors
  - ➤ Daily activities and exercise
  - ➤ Quality of food and menu
  - ➤ Guardrails in bathrooms and beds
  - ➤ Call buttons/direct phone to room
  - ➤ Security guards to block wandering
- Complete application
  - ➤ Medical records
  - ➤ Application package (100+ pages)
  - ➤ Living will and DNR
  - ➤ Funeral home information
- Your contact information
- Payment arrangements
- Emergency contacts at facility
- Palliative and hospice care

Living Arrangements:
Pros and Cons

DIY

Pros:

- Cheaper
- More quality time with elderly family member
- More control over care
- Familiar home environment

Cons:

- Time consuming
- Juggling work and child care
- Retrofitting house with guardrails and stairlifts
- Emotional exhaustion
- Burden of care if something happens

Caregiver

Pros:

- Family member gets to stay home in familiar setting
- Takes burden of elder care off your shoulders
- Doesn't interfere with work or other family duties
- Handles cooking and cleaning for mom and dad
- You don't have to live with your elderly family

Cons:

- Expensive
- Have to still pay both for caregiver and living expenses, like groceries
- Finding a caregiver
- Supervising the care provided
- Managing an employee
- Paying them on time
- Checking cleanliness and care of house

Nursing Home

Pros:

- Elderly family are being taken care of
- Elderly parent's house is empty and can be cleaned out or sold
- No cooking, meals are taken care of
- Less lonely with planned activities and built-in social circle
- Doesn't interfere with work and family duties
- One payment for room and board together

Cons:

- Expensive
- Need to supervise mom and dad are getting adequate care and attention
- Checking quality of food
- Have to visit regularly
- Dealing with management, staff and bureaucracy
- Tons of paperwork
- Emotionally difficult to see parents in an institution

Norman

My father Norman, the subject of my book *The Norman and Phyllis Show*, was eccentric. But when it came to business, and his own elder care planning, he was totally serious.

He had an incredible sense of humor and a gift for gab.

Whenever a stranger recognized him, he would ask if they were a bank teller. Why a bank teller? Because he was a bank robber, he told them. They probably only had seen him, of course, at their teller window. He didn't work Wednesdays, obviously, referring to a time decades ago when banks were closed every Wednesday.

That was Norman. I never knew what he would say. He had a gift for saying the wrong thing to the wrong person at the wrong time, like he did when meeting Barack Obama.

Norman met Obama during a campaign stop for his Senate race in 2004 at Manny's, a famous Chicago deli. When Obama told Norman that he looked familiar, my dad just had to say the unthinkable. "Yeah, I've seen you naked in the locker room of the East Bank Club," a prestigious health club in

Chicago, where they both happened to be members.

In between, Norman and Phyllis were aficionados of Chicago's most famous restaurants – Gibsons, Gene & Georgetti, Carmine's and Tuscany.

He loved to teach the Mexican waiters Yiddish phrases and greetings. They loved him. He tipped them well. They inducted him into "The Golden Tipper's Club."

I always thought insanity was hereditary. I always thought the job of parents was to pass on their craziness to their children or, at least, embarrass them children in public.

What I inherited was Norman's sense of humor and gift for gab. I also inherited his talent for organizing his business affairs.

The First Elderly Parent Needing Care

He was the first of our four parents who needed elder care. He was in such good health, or so it seemed, we expected him to be the last to perish. Instead, he was the first. When he started to fail, it was a complete surprise.

Norman played racquetball until he was eighty and, for just as long, had an eye for the ladies, hanging out daily at the East Bank Club in Chicago, where he lived all of his life. My mother, Phyllis, outlived him, surviving another eight years after their sixty plus years of marriage.

Norman liked to call himself a *shtarker menschen*, Yiddish for a strong man.

It wasn't until he got really sick that I understood his fascination with cardiology. He was an accountant and businessman, fields not even remotely related to medicine.

Norman's Congenital Heart Defect

Norman had a congenital heart defect called Bicuspid Aortic Valve (BAV) disease. A normal aortic valve has three leaflets. The aortic valve of BAV sufferers has only two leaflets. It's the most common congenital heart ailment. Norman's case was typical, right out of a medical textbook.

Norman rarely talked about it, and it didn't stop him from raising a family and living a full life. It wasn't until he was in his mid-70s that doctors noticed some pressure on the aorta, the heart's largest artery, and told him the valve had to be replaced.

He recovered quickly from the surgery within a year and was back at the East Bank Club, his favorite daily haunt, playing racquetball and girl watching, his other favorite pastime.

The new valve held up for another five years.

Norman Totally Loses It

Then, one night, Sara and I waited over an hour at a restaurant for Norman to show up. He came alone. The normally alert Norman had forgotten to bring Phyllis, who he used to bring to this same restaurant nearly every Saturday night for decades. He was confused and ordered breakfast instead of dinner and tried to pay for the bill with an expired credit card.

Still in a state of total shock, I soon learned that he had stopped going to the office and was babbling about nonsense whenever I visited him at home.

The valve was deteriorating. The medication the doctors had given him, Warfarin, was a blood thinner. It also doubled as a rat poison, I later learned. Strong stuff. Probably too strong for Norman at this point.

Norman was losing his mind. The medication was causing him to get dementia.

His office started calling me. "Where's Norman?" they would ask. "What's going on? Why isn't he coming into the office?" I didn't know myself either. I told them I had to find out.

Norman seemed to be out of it. I noticed sometimes he was out of breath. Unusual for my father the champion racquetball player at the East Bank Club.

Finally Taking Legal Control

I called his doctor to find out. Her office wouldn't talk to me. Norman had only authorized my mother, not me, for release of his health care information. But he had an upcoming appointment, and I decided to tag along and bring Phyllis.

While I was waiting at the doctor's office, my mother stepped off the elevator with only her walker and her caregiver. No Norman. He either had forgotten or didn't want to come. We met with the doctor, without Norman, and she confirmed he had complications from the deterioration of his replacement heart valve.

The doctor also agreed to add me as a contact for Norman, so I could get updates from her office.

The next week, Sara and I asked one of Norman's closest friends and his wife to meet us at his house. We wanted to take away his car keys. He was becoming too incoherent to drive. His friend and his wife, Norman's friends since childhood, were taken aback by Norman's mental state. With their help, we managed to get the keys without a peep.

That Saturday, when I came to visit, Norman was lying in bed. The sheets were covered with blood. He was having nose bleeds. There were blood-stained Kleenexes on the floor next to the bed. "It's nothing," he said. "Just a little nose bleed."

I rushed him to the emergency room, where Sara and I sat with him for hours. He was totally in outer space. When the doctors asked him where he was, he answered, "Cleveland." Cleveland? Why Cleveland? He thought he had been taken to a famous heart center there. They asked him who the president was. He didn't know. "But I think his wife is Black," referring to Michelle, First Lady to then-president Barack Obama.

Norman spent a week in the hospital undergoing tests. He started yelling at nurses and threatened to sue everybody in sight, including me, when I came to visit. This was totally out-of-character for the fun-loving and gregarious Norman, who talked to anybody, even strangers, everywhere he went, even at some of Chicago's most famous restaurants.

The hospital sent him to rehab, coincidentally at the same nursing home his mother, Grandma Ida, had been at seven years before. That was on a Friday. Two days later, on Sunday, the nursing home called us and said he had a fever. He had to go back to the hospital.

Norman's Final Days on Life Support

Sara and I rushed back to the same emergency room where his drama had started a week before. It was more than a fever. He was on life support with a breathing tube in his throat. I was shocked to see my dad, so lively and vigorous, attached to machines keeping him alive. He couldn't even breath on his own anymore.

While in intensive care, I had to scramble with my mother to pay the bills. I called the bank. I called his attorney. Nobody would talk to me. Only my mother had power of attorney, and only my mother was on all the bank accounts. My mother noticed that Norman's checking account was almost out of funds. She needed my help.

Before Phyllis was about to write a bad check to the caregiver, I arranged to have her meet me at their bank in downtown Chicago. Her caregiver packed her and her walker up in a taxi. My mother and I met face-to-face with a banker and signed paperwork to add me to the checking accounts.

The banker then transferred funds from Norman's savings into the checking, so I could help pay bills.

I finally had joint control, with Phyllis, of my father's finances to help my mom pay the bills.

Meanwhile, Norman was languishing back in intensive care. Though walker-bound herself, unable to walk on her own, she insisted we take her to see my dad in the hospital.

I got choked up, and it tore my heart apart, when my mom talked to an unconscious Norman about their first date. "He was so handsome when he came down the stairs," she said about her then high school sweetheart, her gnarled hands gripping her walker.

After two weeks, the doctors said they couldn't help Norman anymore. They wanted to move my dad to hospice. The doctor said he was sorry, as he put his hand gently on Phyllis's shoulder.

Unable to breath unaided, my father passed away quietly in the hospital's hospice unit two days later. Sara and I were in the elevator on our way up to visit, when we got the call. He had just died fifteen minutes earlier.

When I got there, I cracked open the door and saw Norman lying in bed, his head cocked to the side on his shoulder. He looked like he was asleep. That was just how I wanted to remember him, asleep after an exhausting racquetball game, or just after a long day of running around the city.

Legal Documents I: Powers of Attorney

Norman's paperwork with complete instructions for his elder care was all in order. He had Powers of Attorney for both property and health care, and a DNR and Living Will.

That didn't surprise me. He was an accountant and CPA all his life, and part of his business was estate planning for wealthy individuals and trust fund "brats" as Norman humorously called them. He knew how to draft powers of attorney.

When the time came, and he started to fail, I had no problem finding everything. We found everything before he died, including his will and an old life insurance policy rolled up with rubber bands, in his safe deposit box.

There was only one problem. I wasn't an agent on any powers of attorney. I wasn't even a successor agent, who steps in when the primary agent is unwilling or unable to perform their duties. My name wasn't actually on any document. The only name left on everything was my mom's. My mom, Phyllis, was left as the sole agent.

By this time, Phyllis was also on the road to dementia. She drifted in and out. I scrambled during the big windows while she was still lucid, working with my parent's attorney, to have her sign new Powers of Attorney from her to me, in other words, designating me as her agent.

The attorney was fantastic. He knew my dad since they were frat brothers in college and carefully walked me through every detail of the process.

Once the notary seal was dry on her Powers of Attorney, I could finally legally help my ailing parents. The attorney was pleased that I handled everything so well and jokingly told me I was practicing law without a license.

The Different Types of Powers of Attorney

Let's review the different types of powers of attorney and how to set up and use them.

This is only a very high-level review of powers of attorney and isn't an exhaustive list of all types of powers of attorney available. We've heard of as many as five different kinds of powers of attorney.

We're only going to review the two powers of attorney – property and health care – we used for taking care of our elderly parents.

For any other power of attorney, we urge you to consult a legal professional. In fact, you should always consult an attorney, preferably one specializing in estate law, even for the two discussed here, when drafting any power of attorney.

> **Any information discussed in this book should not be considered any type of legal advice.**

In addition, estate laws, including those for powers of attorney, vary from state to state. There are a lot of similarities between states, but not for everything. Your attorney can advise on the nuances in your state – another reason to consult an attorney.

So, what is a power of attorney and what "power" does it have?

A power of attorney is an agreement between two parties, allowing one party to act on behalf of another party. The correct terminology is that someone "gives," or "grants," a power of attorney to an "agent." The person granting authority is called the "principal," and the person acting on the principal's behalf is called the "agent."

An agent is sometimes referred to as an Attorney-in-Fact, though the agent doesn't have to be – and usually isn't – actually an attorney. It can be anyone chosen by the principal. It doesn't even have to be a family member. It could be a total stranger, though this isn't a good idea. Obviously, whether a family member or not, the chosen agent should be someone you trust.

In addition to the agent, there should be at least two successor agents listed in case the named agent becomes incapacitated, resigns or is otherwise unable to perform their duties as an agent. There can be more than one successor, listed in order of precedence, to make sure there is always a domino still standing if prior agents start falling.

This was the mistake Norman made when he only named Phyllis, and not me, as the agent with no other successor. We resolved this by creating a Power of Attorney with Phyllis as the principal and myself as the agent.

The first of the two types of powers of attorney we've used is for property. It can be durable or revocable. A durable power of attorney remains in effect when the principal becomes incapacitated, while a revocable power of attorney automatically ends when the principal becomes incompetent.

The principal can still change or revoke a durable power of attorney at any time, as long as they're competent. It just doesn't terminate automatically by itself, like a revocable power of attorney, unless the document expressly has an expiration date.

This also means, obviously, both durable and revocable powers of attorney must be completed and signed while the principal is still lucid and mentally competent.

The power of attorney for property can be general or limited. The powers of attorney we've used list over a dozen possible functions the principal can grant an agent. All are related to some sort of financial transaction, such as selling real estate, trading stocks and bonds, and paying taxes and insurance.

The financial transactions the principal doesn't want to allow should be crossed out. So, for example, if the principal only wants the agent to be able to sell their real estate, and not be able to conduct any other financial transaction, they would cross out every function except the one allowing the sale of real estate.

Sara and I were saddled with houses from both of our parents, and the clause allowing us to sell their homes while they were still in the nursing home was a tremendous help. It was one less thing to clean up and deal with after they passed away. The money from the sale of the homes also helped pay their nursing home costs.

Without a power of attorney granting such authority, unless you jointly own the house with your parents (called "joint tenants with rights of survivorship"), you would have to wait until they died, assuming the will even grants you the house, and even longer if it's tied up in probate.

Health Care Powers of Attorney

The other power of attorney is for health care. The health care power of attorney is usually associated with two other documents: the living will and the Do Not Resuscitate, or DNR.

Each document has its own function. The health care power of attorney is the "who," and the living will, also called an advance directive, is the "what." The health care power of attorney designates who is responsible for decisions about the principal's health, while the living will designates what they can do.

The living will has specific instructions and is more detailed and granular than the DNR. The DNR is very narrow and only provides instructions in case the principal has heart failure or stops breathing.

The DNR is usually a pre-printed form issued by the state with checkboxes and blank lines to fill in rather than a document drafted by an attorney.

The DNR is an agreement between the doctor and the patient. The doctor is responsible for completing the form, and the patient, if they're still able, or their agent named in the health care power of attorney, signs the form. This is why a health care power of attorney is essential if the patient is incompetent and someone else has to sign the form.

Without powers of attorney, handling the financial affairs, or getting care for your elderly parents, can be a nightmare. You end up having to go to court to appoint a conservator, which is a cumbersome process.

While working with the attorney for your elderly parents, you should set up powers of attorney for yourself and your spouse, even if you're young and healthy and think you're invincible and immortal. You never know when you could be incapacitated prematurely yourself by an injury or illness.

Later, when you're older, it can be updated to name your children as your agents. At least, it's already in place and is one less thing your children will have to handle for your own elder care.

It's important to remember powers of attorney are only in force while the principal is still alive. As soon as the principal dies, all powers of attorney become invalid, and the will takes over.

The story of Sara's mother, Eleanor, an important lesson on the importance of having a will, is next. Fortunately, Eleanor signed her will just in time, hours before passing.

Eleanor

Our family always thought Sara's mother, Eleanor, would be the first of our four parents to pass away.

Eleanor lived with several ailments. She suffered from Chronic Lymphocytic Leukemia (CLL) for decades, as well as, diabetes and had back problems walking from numbness in her legs. We all thought she was an emergency room case waiting to happen. Not so.

That honor went to my father, Norman, who died exactly three weeks to the day before Eleanor, after being sick for less than a month.

It was a strange summer for us caring for two critically ill elderly parents at the same time and then arranging back-to-back funerals within weeks of each other.

I was totally dazed and in shock all that summer. Anytime someone called, who I hadn't spoken to in a while, even if not family, I would yell into the phone, "Who died?" before even saying hello.

Unlike other forms of leukemia, CLL isn't fatal. Treatments have vastly improved since Eleanor's time, but even back then, the treatments included only regular, usually monthly, blood transfusions and medication. It was more of an inconvenience than a disability.

It didn't stop Eleanor from living a full and happy life, or being a wildly successful academic.

Eleanor the World-Renowned Academic

Eleanor got a PhD in archaeology at the University of Chicago in the Hyde Park neighborhood where she lived with her husband Sidney, while raising two kids and taking care of a household. Between it all, she was a fabulous cook and made sure dinner was ready every night.

Eleanor presented papers at conferences every year in Europe in her field of Greek and Roman statues. Sidney traveled with her, turning her trips into working vacations.

As a fellow academic, Sid, a professor of civil engineering at the Illinois Institute of Technology (IIT), totally supported her work. They respected each other professionally.

Eleanor used to say she was an archaeologist who didn't dig. Instead, she would spend a month at a time traveling around Europe where she was a celebrity in the antiquities department of every museum and university. Doors would open for the expert from Chicago to conduct her field work with original artifacts.

She was also a big shot at the Oriental Institute, a world-renowned antiquities museum that happened to be around the corner from her in Hyde Park. She did research and helped catalog their acquisitions.

Eleanor lit up any time she talked about ancient empires. Her passion showed through in her encyclopedic knowledge of classical history. When I would ask her a simple question about some ancient wall or building that I had seen in my own travels, she would answer with a detailed half-hour lecture only an enthralled academic could deliver. I was amazed by not only her enthusiasm and energy but also her vast knowledge.

I once asked Eleanor, "What about the circular wall around the old city of Nicosia in Cyprus?" I thought I could stump her with some obscure piece of archaeological trivia from a place I visited on a business trip. No way. Eleanor had never been to Cyprus but still knew all about its many ruins and treated me to one of her famous half-hour lectures. She was on a first name basis with every medieval Cypriot conqueror and knew exactly who built that wall and when.

Eleanor was too busy with her career to be bothered with, what were in her mind, trivial matters like estate planning. Sid and her were tremendous savers. Sid did well enough with his endowed chair at IIT for them to be comfortable. They put away enough for retirement from Sid's pensions and their IRAs, yet were still able to go to Europe every summer, where Eleanor's trips were covered by university grants.

Incomplete Estate Planning

Savings for their retirement wasn't the issue. The problem was their wills. They seemed to never be complete. Every time Sara asked, she got a half answer or incomplete and unsigned documents. She got a parade of excuses. The attorney was busy and couldn't talk, Eleanor would say. She had to meet a deadline for her next paper or grant proposal. She was getting ready for a presentation at an important conference in Europe.

Then when Sara asked about bank accounts, she got, instead, a list of academic and archaeological organizations to contact when she died. The list of bank accounts, like the will, was incomplete and scattered. Posthumous prestige was more important than posthumous planning.

Sara finally got, what she thought, was a complete list of bank accounts by keeping after her parents.

After Eleanor died, Sara got letters from banks about abandoned accounts. Eleanor had opened, and forgotten about, a few small accounts with extra money for her travels and purchases of beautiful but expensive coffee table books she loved about obscure archaeological sites known only to her.

Eleanor, like many people, couldn't face her own mortality. She was totally normal. Some – in fact, many – people just can't bring themselves to do their own will. It's too painful. It reminds them of their death, something they would rather forget or, at least, put off.

But it can't be ignored, no matter how hard we try. Nature always wins and chooses when and where to act on its terms, not ours.

Eleanor's illnesses finally caught up with her during the last two years of her life. The numbness in her legs caused her to start falling often, sometimes severe enough to end up in emergency rooms and then rehab for a few weeks.

Sara got Eleanor a medical alert device, which she never used, and we eventually had to return. She fell once while Sid was at work and sat on the floor all day until he got back home.

Besides the falls, she needed more care for her CLL and diabetes. She seemed to have one problem after another. After a while, we couldn't keep track anymore of how many times we visited her in the hospital or rehab. We helped Sid take care of errands and shopping for the house, since she was hardly at home. She was in the middle of a big project for the Oriental Institute, which she had to put on hold.

Eleanor Signs the Will on Her Deathbed

In the end, it wasn't CLL that did her in. Another villain, a very rare cancer called Merkel Cell Carcinoma took her life after about only a month. Merkel is a skin cancer that causes painful blisters on the legs and arms. At the time, there was no cure. It was completely fatal.

Eleanor suffered tremendously the last few weeks of her life. The blisters were big and nasty and unspeakably painful. They eventually covered her legs and swelled up her feet.

Though Eleanor was only briefly in rehab, she got a taste of nursing home life during her last days.

After her last visit to rehab, she went back to the University of Chicago hospital near her house. The doctors told us Eleanor had only days to live. Sara's brother Jeremy flew in from San Diego. Sara,

Jeremy and Sid and I spent a few anxious days in the hospital, watching her slip away.

The will had recently been completed but still wasn't signed.

Eleanor and Sid's attorney, who luckily also lived in Hyde Park, rushed over with a briefcase full of papers. He hastily found notaries in the hospital, and Sara found witnesses, and went to Eleanor's bedside with the documents. He carefully handed her each page to sign, pacing himself between her gasps of pain.

As soon as the attorney was done and left, hours later Eleanor slipped into a coma from which she never awoke.

The attorney said he had never had anyone sign a will on their deathbed. He said it would be a story for his fellow estate attorneys.

It was a drama worthy of Hollywood, except it was real life.

Legal Documents II: Wills

When most people think of wills, they picture a wealthy family seated together in a huge stateroom ornately decorated with family heirlooms in a luxurious mansion. In front of the gathering is some official looking person, possibly an attorney, sitting in front of the gathering reading from a list of who gets what.

This aunt gets the Bentley. That son gets the race horses. This daughter gets the country estate, and some mysterious uncle gets the rest of the family fortune. What remains is divvyed up among a bunch of pissed off high-society heirs who expected a piece of the cake but only got breadcrumbs from their deceased multibillionaire family's estate.

Wills can have clauses doling out specific pieces of property, especially for unique, exotic, or valuable items. But generally, wills aren't full of Hollywood drama. They aren't that exciting. They're actually quite boring.

As with the previous discussion about powers of attorney, any information provided here shouldn't be construed as legal advice.

A will is a legal document and should be drafted and reviewed by your attorney.

What Exactly is a Will?

A will is basically just the deceased's instructions how to divide up their property after they die. It's usually expressed as a percentage of the monetary value of the property in the deceased's estate. That property is usually financial in nature, such as cash, bank accounts, investment accounts like 401Ks and IRAs or brokerage accounts with stocks and bonds and, of course, real estate.

When someone dies, their powers of attorney disappear. They terminate and their will takes over.

Think of a power of attorney as for the living, while the will is for the deceased.

Put another way, the deceased ceases to exist not only physically but also as a property owner. Their property becomes part of what is called their "estate." If John Doe is listed as the owner of whatever, say, a checking account, the owner is now the "estate of John Doe."

So, for example, the deceased's spouse might get such and such percentage of their estate, while siblings and kids each get another percentage, maybe equally divided among them. In some cases, depending on the deceased's wishes, part of the estate may be given to someone outside the family, or to a charity or other organization.

Without a will, the deceased is called "intestate." In that case, dividing the inheritance is governed by state law, depending on residency of the deceased and the location of the property. For personal property, for example, that would be the laws of the state where the deceased had legal residency. For real estate, on the other hand, if located in another state, the laws of the state where the property is located apply.

Inheritance Laws Vary by State

Inheritance laws vary from state to state, but they often follow a similar pattern. They all have a hierarchy of heirs starting with the surviving spouse, then their descendants, followed by parents and siblings. For example, the surviving spouse may get the entire estate if there are no descendants. If there are children, the spouse only gets half and the other half is divided equally among the children. If the deceased had no spouse or children, then the parents and brothers and sisters would be the heirs.

Had Eleanor not signed her will a few hours before passing, she would have been intestate, and then her family's problems with her inheritance would just be the beginning. Her assets would have been tied up in probate, which can be costly and time consuming, before Sara's family would receive anything.

Your elderly family members should always have a will, even if they have little or no property. It's a good idea for the whole family, not just you and your spouse, to also have wills. You're never too young to have a will. Family members don't pass in any order or on our schedule, despite their age or their state of health.

Joint Tenants with Rights of Survivorship

Ideally, you should try to own all property jointly with your parents. The legal term is "joint tenants with rights of survivorship." Understandably, this isn't always realistic. It depends, of course, on your family's financial situation and how well family members get along with each other.

This means you would be a co-owner, not just a co-signer, on all bank accounts, whether checking or savings, and all investment accounts, such as brokerage or stock and bond accounts, as well as, titles to real estate. For IRAs and 401Ks, you should be listed as a beneficiary.

Banks distinguish between co-signers and co-owners. A co-signer can only write and sign checks on, or make withdrawals from, a checking account, for example. They don't control the account. Only a full owner controls the account. In the event the owner of the account passes, a co-signer doesn't have access to the account any longer.

If you're just a co-signer, you would have to go through probate first to take over the account, again, assuming you're in the will. In joint tenancy, on the other hand, ownership of accounts passes directly to the surviving owner, or owners, without needing a will or having to go through probate.

IRAs and 401Ks should always have you listed as beneficiaries, so they go to you directly, instead of through probate. If there is no beneficiary, your deceased parent's IRAs and 401Ks, which they saved through hard work, winds up in probate.

Another way to sidestep probate is to put property in a living trust. A living trust is a document that transfers ownership of your parent's assets to the trust. Since the property is legally owned by the trust, not your parents, it isn't considered part of their estate and, as a result, not part of probate. A trust also provides privacy, since the list of its assets isn't available to the public.

The party setting up the trust, your parents or other elderly family members, for example, would be the trustee, meaning they control the assets in the trust during their lifetime. The trustee names a successor trustee, who are the heirs inheriting the assets in the trust directly when they pass away.

Your elderly family members should still have a will, even if everything is jointly owned, or held in trust, to make sure everybody inherits what they were promised.

Parties to a Will

Like powers of attorney, wills have more than one party. A will typically has four parties, a testator, beneficiaries, an executor, and witnesses.

The testator, or testatrix for a woman, is the person making the will and who designates beneficiaries, the legal term for their heirs or those who will inherit their assets. The executor, named in the will, carries out the will's instructions.

Finally, witnesses observe the testator signing the will and then sign it themselves, attesting to its validity.

In Eleanor's case, Sara called two of her friends to come to the hospital to act as emergency witnesses. They were at her bedside while she signed the will.

The executor can be compared to a project manager who oversees implementation of the will. It can be an attorney or even a family member named as a beneficiary. Nothing prevents an executor from also being a beneficiary. Of course, if this is an issue, consult an attorney for guidance on who should be parties to the will.

Also, like powers of attorney, there should be backups in case named parties pass away or just become incompetent. The will, like the power of attorney, should designate a list of successor executors and beneficiaries in hierarchical order. An example would be the testator's spouse, followed by their siblings or children and maybe then a charity if all the living beneficiaries in the chain have passed away.

The Legal Processes for Estates

You should begin the legal proceedings as soon as possible after your family member passes. Again, as with everything else related to estates, the laws and procedures vary by state or locality. You should check with your attorney and, in fact, should have him or her handle the filing of the paperwork with the probate division of your local circuit court.

The most important document to start legal proceedings is the death certificate. The funeral home can provide a few to start and then more can be purchased directly from the vital records department of your local government.

You can't do anything legally or financially without a death certificate. You can't execute the will or go to probate, at all, for example, and you can't make a claim as a beneficiary on any IRA or 401K accounts. You can't redeem a life insurance policy, either, without a death certificate. It's basically proof of death, and everybody, from lawyers and bankers to investment and brokerage account managers, will ask for it.

The Ins and Outs of Probate

The deadline for filing with the probate court is often around 30 days. After that date, there could be fines or loss of rights as an executor. This is why it's best to have your attorney handle the process to move it along faster and avoid glitches and missteps.

The probate court will need the will and an inventory of assets and, of course, a death certificate, among other documents provided by your attorney. The purpose of probate, besides organizing distribution of the deceased's assets, is to allow creditors, or others, with claims against the estate, including the IRS for back taxes, to get their share of the pie.

If you're aware of any back taxes – from local property taxes up to federal income taxes – pay them while your parents are still alive. The IRS can muck up probate if unpaid taxes show up. The same for any outstanding debts. Anything paid off before death, doesn't end up in probate.

Since part of the purpose of probate is to allow claims to be made against the estate, the list of assets filed with the court is public record. To avoid standing financially naked in public, make sure to keep as much as possible out of the inventory of assets through joint ownership of accounts and trusts.

Your parents might even consider, depending on their financial situation and your relationship with them, gifting assets to the family while they're still alive. This avoids not only wills and probate but may even help with taxes. Consult your accountant if this is even possible or makes sense in your situation.

The probate court will issue a Letter of Testamentary to the executor after all documents have been filed and the process is complete. Our experience has been the process can take from two weeks up to six months, depending on how quickly, and complete, the documents are filed with the court. If the estate is complex, it may take longer, sometimes years.

Banks and financial institutions require the Letter of Testamentary, besides the death certificate, before they allow access to any of your deceased family's accounts listed in probate. The executor can't get past the security guard at the bank, let alone transact any business, without these documents.

No Assets? No Probate? No Problem

If there are no assets to declare, there is no probate and the will is just filed with the circuit court as a matter of record. The estate can remain open for claims for two years, depending on your state's laws, and is then closed from further claims. Under probate, the estate is closed when the executor finishes his or her duties under the terms of the will.

Without a will, the probate court appoints someone to administer the estate and distribute assets under the state's succession laws. The court will issue a Letter of Administration to the administrator, similar to the Letter of Testamentary it gives an executor of a will, to handle financial transactions and to distribute the estate's assets.

Taxes, Life Insurance and Other Fun Stuff

This has been a very high-level overview and shouldn't be considered a complete review of all aspects of estates and wills. We've never had to contest a will and have only heard of one situation where a mentally disturbed person willed everything to a church without telling her kids, leaving them in legal limbo to fight it out for themselves.

We also haven't touched at all on any tax issues related to estates or talked about life insurance. If your parent's estate is large enough to be impacted by estate taxes, which could be either state or federal, or both, consult your attorney and accountant for advice.

The proceeds from life insurance are usually tax free but, as with everything else mentioned here, double check with your attorney and accountant.

Life insurance can be tricky if the policies are so old the company issuing them has gone out of business. Sometimes, the original company was simply acquired by another company, and the old policy is still in force with the new company. It might take some research to find out, but don't just assume an old policy showing up out of nowhere in some drawer is automatically invalid or worthless. If the policy was bought a long time ago, it might just be valid under another company name.

This concludes our discussion of documents needed for elder care. Everything should be assembled while your family members are still alive and mentally aware. Again, these are the powers of attorney, living wills, lists of assets, life insurance policies, if there are any, and, of course, the will, the master instructions after mom or dad pass away.

Next, we're going to tell the story of my mother, Phyllis, and Sara's father, Sidney, and how we helped them with funeral planning – years before they passed.

Documents Checklist

- Powers of Attorney (POA)
  - ➢ Property
  - ➢ Health Care
  - ➢ Name of principal
  - ➢ Name of agent and successors
- Living Will
- Do Not Resuscitate (DNR)
- List of bank accounts
- List of assets
  - ➢ Pensions
  - ➢ IRAs/401Ks and their beneficiaries
  - ➢ Investment/brokerage accounts
  - ➢ Real estate
- Life insurance
- Wills and trust
  - ➢ Name of executor and successors
  - ➢ Names of heirs
- Name of estate attorney
- Death certificate
- Probate documents
  - ➢ Letter of Testamentary
  - ➢ Letter of Administration (if intestate)

Phyllis

My mother, Phyllis, was already starting to decline just before her husband, Norman, passed away. She was already using a walker with footies covered by split tennis balls, put there by the caregiver Norman had hired, to make it easier for her to get around.

She followed the traditional path of elderly care outlined in this book, starting with Norman caring for her at home, then bringing in a caregiver to help, and finally ending up in a nursing home.

I profile my mother extensively in my previous book, *The Norman and Phyllis Show*, a memoir about my eccentric parents. I survived them long enough to wind up caring for them both in old age.

Phyllis was a stereotypical Jewish mother, right out of central casting. She was neurotic, a bit crazy, and at a baseline level of hysteria all the time. Beneath her constant screaming and yelling at Norman was a loving mother who cared for me more than I ever realized at the time.

Taking care of her in old age was the least I could do to pay her back.

My mother was as goofy as Norman in public, always saying the wrong thing to the wrong person at the wrong time. Bowel movements and bodily functions were her favorite topic of conversation. She told every waiter, when asked whether she wanted soup or salad, that soup gave her gas, pressing her fingers on her abdomen for emphasis.

They were the uncrowned royalty of Chicago's restaurant scene, forced to go out to eat, since Phyllis was a lousy cook. They would have starved to death otherwise.

Together, they were like a match thrown at gasoline. Phyllis was the burning match tossed at Norman's combustible wacky fuel.

As already discussed in the chapter about caregivers, Living Arrangements I: Caregivers, Phyllis's caregiver started only coming during the day. After Norman died, when the caregiver found Phyllis on the floor two mornings in a row, we asked her to move in, which she did.

Everything was fine until the caregiver asked me if her son could move in. I agreed. When Phyllis was lucid, she had met and liked the caregiver's son.

Everything was still fine for a while, until we started getting complaints about the son's smoking and erratic behavior. As it turned out, the caregiver had wanted her son there to help her, since she was getting older and starting to fail herself. This wasn't obvious to us, at first, but became increasingly apparent as we got more complaints about the son.

Phyllis escaped from the house once in the middle of the night. Somehow, she unlocked the front door, got down the elevator, and slipped past the building's doorman – incredibly, without her walker – and security cameras out onto the street.

Phyllis Needs Skilled Nursing Care

This was the first sign that she needed to be moved into a nursing home. At least in a nursing home, there were locked doors and a reception area with staff to prevent residents from wandering off.

It was only an alert cop, who saw a barefoot elderly woman walking dazed in her nightgown on the street, that saved her. The cop took her to a nearby emergency room, which called me at 4:30 in the morning to tell me to pick her up.

We got her a bracelet, which she couldn't remove, with her name, my name and phone number, as a stopgap measure in case she tried to run away again.

At that point, it was obvious the caregiver could no longer provide adequate care. Her dementia had already advanced to the point where she couldn't talk, didn't know my name anymore and was completely unaware of her surroundings.

When I made the decision to move Phyllis, I worked the numbers. The total cost each month for the caregiver plus groceries, utilities and condo expenses ended up being the same as the all-in cost for a double room at the nursing home we had chosen. With the nursing home, I only had to make a single payment each month, since it included room and board. There were no extra fees, except for an occasional haircut, which was pennies compared to the cost of the nursing home.

Between her monthly social security checks and savings from Norman's 401Ks and IRAs, I was able to pay for the caregiver and later the nursing home.

I moved her into a small private nursing home near us in Chicago that was eventually bought by a large nursing home chain based in the area. In her demented state, she thought she was on a cruise or at a resort. She had no idea where she was.

The details of my mother's nursing home experience, and her death from Covid, have already been discussed in the chapter on nursing homes, Living Arrangements II: Nursing Homes.

Paperwork Already in Place

By the time, Phyllis was in the nursing home, powers of attorneys and wills were already in place. Norman had done an excellent job of putting together a clear and understandable will. The only documents I had to straighten out, as discussed previously, were the powers of attorney.

Having the paperwork in place eased the sale of her house, which I did as soon as she moved out. My parents weren't pack rats, so there wasn't tons of stuff to go through and throw away. But it still took a couple of months to clean out the house, including removing all the furniture, do a few minor repairs, and splash a coat of paint on the walls to make it presentable for the realtor.

We put the money from the sale of the house into her savings to help cover the cost of the nursing home.

With the legal paperwork out of the way, the caregiver and nursing home taken care of, and her house sold, there was only one more thing to do – plan for her future funeral.

We learned our lesson, when Norman passed away eight years earlier. His was the first funeral we had to arrange completely on our own, from scratch. Somehow my parents had missed this step in their elder care planning. They had bought cemetery plots for our two families, only a few years early, coincidentally, mostly because of Eleanor's declining health, but then stopped just short of planning a complete funeral. They didn't see the need. They thought it would be years off in the future. They were wrong.

When Norman passed, we chose the same local Jewish funeral home he had used for his mother and grandparents. Selecting the funeral home, at least, was easy. Weinstein was well-known and respected with locations throughout the Chicago area. They also worked directly with the cemetery where we had bought the plots. That was the only easy part.

We spent a few hours going over all the details, from picking the casket and the room where the service would be held to scheduling and booking the shiva – the Jewish visitation after the funeral – and working with the rabbi conducting the service.

After we did it once, we had a template for a sample funeral we could reuse for the remaining family members, including ourselves. That may sound cold and callous, on the surface, but the worst time to arrange a funeral is right after someone dies. You're on emotional overdrive, often to exhaustion, and your head just isn't in a place to be planning anything, let alone a major event like a funeral.

When Eleanor died, three weeks to the day after Norman, we went to the same funeral home and just retraced the details they already had on file for Norman. It took us a lot less time and aggravation to arrange her funeral. We were already prepared.

Template in hand, we could easily pre-plan both Phyllis's and Sidney's funerals, and then later, our own.

Funerals are always emotionally difficult. The ease of pre-planning doesn't take away from the pain of mourning. But it's one less thing to take care of during that difficult time.

We talk next about the last elderly person we cared for, Sara's father Sidney and then about how we planned his and Phyllis's funerals in advance.

Sidney

Sara's father Sidney was the seventh, and last, elderly family member we cared for.

Sidney was the most difficult of the bunch. We used to say the other six were training for Sid. He was more than a handful. He fought every offer of help. He was in total denial about aging. He was belligerent and combative, kicking and screaming until he became too weak to fight a few weeks before he passed.

Sid thought his condition was temporary. He honestly thought, until the day he died, he would get out of his wheelchair, walk out of the nursing home, and drive home and go back to work.

"There's a lot of sick people here," he used to say from his wheelchair in the nursing home. "But I'm fine."

Everybody else was old and decrepit. Not Sid. Everybody else always had a problem. Not Sid. He was delusional even as he sat immobile in a wheelchair. He thought he was still decades younger.

At first, that was the case. Sid was fine right after his wife Eleanor had passed away. He was still able to drive to the grocery store and cook for himself. He still kept the house up. He was even dating here and there. He was able to live on his own and take care of himself. On the surface, he was the man about town, the poster child for independent elder living.

That was until his stroke two years later.

Sid Has a Stroke

It wasn't a debilitating stroke, but it was bad enough to affect his walking and, for a while, his speech. His speech recovered. His walking did not. He eventually stopped slurring his words. His walking, in fact, got progressively worse.

After being rushed to the hospital, he went to rehab at a nursing home in downtown Chicago. Sara laid down the law. He either had to have 24-hour live-in care, or had to move to a nursing home. He chose the caregiver.

Sid was forced to retire and had to give up his first love, teaching classes. He wasn't physically able to stand in front of a classroom anymore. He had to turn over his course load to a colleague.

We then had to take over his finances, paying his bills and moving everything from handwritten checks to online and automatic payments. Though

Sid was an engineer and had strong technical skills, he was still stuck in the brick-and-mortar world. The world of online banking and bill pay was beyond him. He was more comfortable writing checks. That ended with his stroke.

The caregiver was a middle-aged Polish woman who was a friend of the Polish cleaning lady both Sara and Sid used to clean their homes. She only worked Monday through Friday, staying overnight at the house all week. She had a friend who covered for her on Saturday and Sunday.

Sid and her hit it off, and everything went well for a few more years. Then the weekend caregiver suddenly disappeared. She had packed up and went back to Poland without telling anyone, even her friend the weekday caregiver. Sara had to scramble to replace her at the last minute.

Then the problems with the weekend caregivers started. Sara went through several agencies to find someone. There was the obese woman from Eastern Europe, another who hid in the dining room to avoid work and a few other unmentionable characters who passed through, until Sara settled on a pleasant middle-aged Polish man who had another job during the week.

Since the first two caregivers were friends, they talked a lot, including about their pay. When the weekday caregiver giver found out how much the weekend caregiver was making, the weekday caregiver complained to Sara about her pay. After that, Sara made sure the weekday and weekend caregivers didn't know how much each other was being paid.

Sid's Car is Taken Away

Then there was the car. Sid got a letter in the mail from the state Department of Motor Vehicles (DMV), revoking his license because of his stroke. Apparently, the doctor who diagnosed the stroke had reported it to the DMV.

Sid was incensed. That couldn't be. How dare them, he yelled, as he waved the cane he now needed for walking in the air. Don't they know I can still drive? My driving is fine. I'll show them, he thought.

And show them he did, as he spectacularly failed the road test at his local DMV facility. The test car was rigged. The tester must not like me. The system is corrupt. And so on and so on. We never heard the end of it.

Sid thought he was smarter than the DMV and was going to beat the system. He scheduled another test at another facility. When he got there, the tester was the same guy from his first failed test.

He stomped out and refused to take the test, saying the DMV was conspiring against him.

The third time wasn't a charm. He had the caregiver take him to another facility in a distant suburb. The tester was someone new who didn't know him. He still failed. He finally realized he couldn't drive anymore and gave us the car. Thousands of dollars in repairs later, it was drivable again. He had apparently stopped doing even routine maintenance on the car.

Even before the stroke, his hot temper flared behind the wheel. He tailgated wherever he could, then yelled to himself in the car. They didn't know how to drive. They were all too slow.

Sid knew how to push every one of Sara's buttons, bringing her, at times, to tears. He refused any suggestion to make his life easier. Instead, he waited until everything was forced on him against his will. He was totally reactive instead of proactive. He was in total denial.

When Sid was living alone, Sara got him a medical alert device to wear around his neck. He refused to use it. She ended up cancelling the service and returning the device. Fortunately, he never fell while still living alone.

When she suggested he move into a one-story condo or house to avoid walking up four flights of stairs, he refused. He had stairlifts installed instead. As his hands got shakier, and getting up and down from the seat got more difficult, he couldn't even manage the stairlifts. He stayed in his bedroom on the top floor with the TV blaring. He also refused to get a hearing aid.

Sid's walking, if it could be called that, got worse. It got so bad, the caregiver had to strap a belt around his waist, like a leash, to get him to the dinner table. He moved like a tin soldier, his legs stiff, in measured steps, the caregiver holding his belt, barely making it to the dining room without falling.

Sid had an accomplice. The caregiver, afraid of losing her job, covered up his failings.

Sid was strong. He only had one kidney, the other removed ten years earlier because of a suspicious growth, which luckily, wasn't cancer.

When Sara showed him a nursing home, the same one where Phyllis was living, he was cordial and polite to the manager and staff. They rolled out the red carpet for him. He even saw Phyllis and said hello, though I'm not sure in her demented state she even remembered or recognized Sid.

It took a few hours for the caregiver to bundle up Sid and his wheelchair in her car to meet us at the nursing home in Skokie. When we got back home, he turned nasty. He unleashed a barrage of angry insults at Sara and made her cry.

How dare her consider such a thing. He was fine, he said from his wheelchair. He didn't need any stinking nursing home. He wouldn't budge.

But, as I always say, nature always wins. Nature always forces its hand. Aging and illness don't care what we think. They work on their own schedule, not ours.

Sid Gets Covid

Covid arrived, and one morning, the caregiver. saw Sid's face droop and one side of his body paralyzed. She thought he had another stroke and called an ambulance. They tested him in the emergency room. It wasn't a stroke, at all. It was Covid.

Sid would later get Covid again two more times – and would survive – both times at the nursing home where he ended up. Sid was strong. He seemed indestructible.

Off to rehab again, this time Warren Barr in River North a fancy neighborhood, as the name implies, just north of the Chicago River. Sid was there a month. He complained about the food, the service, the staff, whatever he could complain about. Sid was never happy – privately. He complained to us constantly. He was charming and effervescent in public, whiny and brooding to his family in private.

Along the way, he started to go in and out of dementia. He had days he was totally lucid, and then other days, when he pulled random nonsense out of the air. He was already a lifelong paranoid, and dementia made it worse.

A month later, when rehab ended, and Sara had to move him to a nursing home, I helped her move him to the same nursing home where my mother had been. Phyllis had already passed away a year earlier. Instead of the Skokie facility he had visited, they put him in a newly acquired facility nearby in Northbrook, another suburb north of Chicago, still close enough for us to visit regularly. No more long trips into the city.

We still don't know where Sid caught Covid, since he never left the house. The weekday caregiver, the only one to leave the house to run errands and get groceries, got tested immediately and was negative.

The weekend caregiver refused to get tested, and Sara let him go. We helped the weekday caregiver get a new job, and she moved on to care for another elderly person, this time, it turned out, someone also Polish and Polish-speaking.

The real fun began when Sid moved into the nursing home.

Sid Versus the Nursing Home

The complaints started as soon as he arrived. They were endless. Nothing was ever good enough for Sid.

Sid complained about the food. Though the meals were decent, he never got used to the institutional food at the nursing home. He preferred the caregiver's home-cooked meals. Besides the food, he complained about the service, which could be spotty, at times, because of staff turnover, but was generally pretty good.

Sid complained about the other residents, most of whom were too disabled or zonked out to be anything other than friendly. "There's too many Russians here," he said. "I can't talk to anyone."

The home was in an area where many Russian émigrés lived. They were mostly Jews allowed to leave the Soviet Union in the 1970s, some of whom never learned to speak English. To accommodate those residents, they had some Russian-speaking staff. There were even ads for the nursing home in

Russian on a local ethnic radio station. But the place was hardly a Russian ghetto. It reflected the diversity of Chicago and its suburbs.

It was just an excuse for Sid to be anti-social and grumpy. We made sure he had a single room. He couldn't get along with a roommate, even if he tried, and he wouldn't try. They weren't good enough for him, or at least, not his intellectual equal.

Of course, when we came to visit, we caught him having fun playing bingo with the Russian babushkas and other residents. He smiled as the numbers were read in English and then Russian. He was the life of the party in the day room. Everybody loved Sid. They had great things to say about him.

The combination of dementia and paranoia was scary. Sid was fine during the day, but when the sun went down, he came out to play.

Shortly after he arrived, he called us every ten to fifteen minutes several nights in a row right after sundown. "They're trying to kill me. You've got to get me out of here." He forgot that he had just called and kept calling repeatedly until a nurse saw him and put the phone down.

Once during a shift change, as the staff was going off duty, he called us in a panic. "The rats are leaving the ship."

Eventually, Sid had to be put on medication to stop the delusions.

Sid still wasn't satisfied. He demanded to talk to the manager of the facility. He wouldn't talk to just anybody. The rest of the staff were mere mortals. They were beneath him. An award-winning academic and former senior executive of a prestigious local university, he felt he should be speaking only to someone at his level – the boss.

Sid had an endowed chair in civil engineering at the Illinois Institute of Technology (IIT) and was a world-renowned expert on concrete. During his stellar academic career over five decades at IIT, he had also served a term as the university's provost.

Sid felt greatness, like himself, should only speak with greatness. His only peer at the facility was the top dog. They met, and the manager listened politely and took notes. He knew how to humor Sid. He too had been in management long enough to know how to handle difficult residents. Sid was no match for the nursing home director.

Sid complained that we weren't calling. We raised the volume on his phone. Problem solved. He couldn't work the radio. The knobs were too small. He couldn't find his station. We got him a dementia radio, specially designed for people with dementia. It had large buttons, an on-off switch he couldn't miss and preset radio stations for the classical music he loved. Problem solved.

"Get me out of here," he said every time we visited. When Sara's brother and his wife, Jeremy and Lisa, came to town two or three times a year, he started with the same routine. "Where is grandpa going to live?" He wanted to spend six months of the year with us, and six months with Jeremy and Lisa. No way. First, he needed skilled care we couldn't provide and, second, neither of us had a room for him. We couldn't put up either with his constant comments and complaining about everything.

Sid also battled loneliness. He outlived all his friends and family. It wasn't easy for him every time he heard about the occasional passing of another colleague, friend or family member.

Cleaning Out Sid's House

Meanwhile, as soon as Sid moved into the nursing home, we started to clean out his house. Both he and Eleanor were professional pack rats. There were rooms packed with books, academic papers from the beginning of time, engineering tools, heavy machinery for woodworking in the basement

– he planned to use in a retirement that never came – and memorabilia saved from when Sara and Jeremy were infants. There was even a broken violin from some forgotten ancestor back in Russia and paint brushes from their uncle the painter, many of whose paintings were on their walls and had to be taken down and stored.

Junk haulers came so often for pickups, they got to know us personally. They became like family.

We learned from Sara's parents that human beings normally accumulate stuff as they get older, and if they're pack rats, the piles just keep getting bigger the longer they live. It still took a couple of months just to clean out my parent's house, who were minimalists and not pack rats, at all.

If you're angry at your parents for all the stuff they've left you with, think about what you might be leaving your kids. Your kids, just like you with your parents, aren't interested in their parent's, meaning your, excess baggage. The quickest way to get kids to resent their parents is to leave them with tons of stuff they don't want or need.

Remember, nobody wants your stuff. Get rid of it while you're still living.

Of course, when Sara suggested her parents get rid of things and clean out the house as they got older and sicker, she met with stiff resistance, of course, and just stopped asking.

Between clearing out all the stuff they accumulated and making repairs they neglected, it took two years to prepare the house for sale. In the meantime, the air conditioning suddenly broke down and the rooftop unit needed to be replaced.

Then, there were repairs to the heating system, concrete work and fencing, carpeting, removal of shelving, new closet doors and a splash of fresh paint.

The heavy woodworking equipment had to be broken down to get through the door. The hauler needed three people to take the machinery apart. They also disposed of hazardous chemicals they found in the workroom. It was a nightmare.

The stairlifts also had to be torn out. None were easy jobs. Some, like removing the stairlifts, left nails in the staircase that had to be removed.

We had to come down to Hyde Park from Skokie almost every week, anywhere from an hour to two-hour drive, depending on Chicago's brutal traffic, sometimes spending the night to let in workmen in the morning. It turned into a part-time gig, except instead of making money, it cost money.

Back at the nursing home, Sid slowly declined. Sara put him on palliative care, as I had done for my mother. They checked on him regularly and made sure, among other things, he was getting adequate care and attention. They also checked if he was taking the right meds, not too much or too little. After a while, Sid didn't recognize the visitors, even though they sent the same person each time, and he even forgot they had visited when we asked him the next day.

Sid's Misadventures at the Doctor

While still on palliative care, Sid sometimes had to go to a doctor. Most of the time, it was routine. Either the nursing home, or Sara, would arrange for a medical van to pick him up, take him to the doctor, drop him off, then come back later to pick him up to take him back to the nursing home.

Sometimes, I had to go along, when Sara wasn't available. Again, most of the time, he was quiet and well-behaved the entire time, during the trips to and from, and at, the doctor's office.

On two occasions, it was a nightmare.

Once, while waiting for the doctor in an examining room, he started moaning loudly, so loudly that a nurse peeked in to see what was going on. He calmed down and then the neurologist walked in.

Sid was totally out of it. He failed her verbal dementia test, a few simple questions about himself and the day's events. He didn't know the correct date or day of the week, where he lived or even who was president.

At another doctor, after the visit, while waiting for the medical van, he started pounding on the armrests of his wheelchair. "I've have to go to the bathroom." I told him the van would be there in a minute. "No," he raised his voice, still pounding on the armrests. "I have to go now." He insisted.

I had to wheel him into a public bathroom down the hall. It was a multi-story medical office building. People walked by us in the hall. No one helped. Getting him through the bathroom door was my first challenge.

Then I had to wheel him into a stall. Fortunately, there was a handicapped stall. I wheeled him in and shut the door. I had to lift him out of the wheelchair and pull off his diaper. It was already stinky and full of poo. He was heavy, between 180 and 200 pounds. I had to make sure he didn't fall – the last thing I needed was to have to call an ambulance for a broken bone. I placed my foot against his to brace him, putting my arm around his waist and lowering him onto the toilet.

I heard him do his business. He was quiet. He didn't say a word. He was able to reach the toilet paper to wipe himself on his own. I then lifted him, again bracing him with my foot and my arm around his waist to keep him from falling. He pulled up his pants and sat back down back in the wheelchair. I then called the medical van to pick him up and the ordeal was finally over.

I've never had to change a baby's diaper, since we never had children. I was paid back with the honor of having to change diapers for the elderly instead.

"Take Me Home! Get Me Out of Here"

Sid never stopped badgering us about going back home, even as he continued to deteriorate both physically and mentally. The palliative care turned into hospice care and the service at the nursing home seemed to get worse at the same time.

Sara started meeting regularly with the director and the staff to check up on his care. The nursing home, like many after Covid, was chronically understaffed. They had to hire part-timers and contractors to meet their staffing needs.

They put up guardrails on both sides of the bed and padding on the floor to keep him from falling or, at least, from hurting himself, when he inevitably did fall, usually on his way to the bathroom.

155

Then suddenly once when Jeremy and Lisa visited, he was listless. He was silent. His eyes were closed, and he sat crumpled in a wheelchair, his bony shoulders poking through the sweater covering his emaciated frame. He had lost a considerable amount of weight in recent months.

Normally, Jeremy would talk to Sid about current events, about the kids, or whatever might catch Sid's attention. He would listen, throwing in an odd comment or two, before going into his "take me home" rant. This time he didn't respond. We missed the fighting spirit that we had gotten used to.

We all knew the end was near. We just didn't realize how close it was.

Sid's Last Days

He stopped eating and drinking. He was a bag of bones laying on his back, eyes closed, staring at the ceiling.

The hospice nurse told Sara, when he stopped eating and drinking, his throat would close, and he would pass within five days.

On the fourth day, when Sara and I visited him, he opened one eye, the only one he had the strength

156

to open, and he gestured for me to come by his side.

Sid reached for my hand with his two bony hands and held tight. It was very spooky. He didn't say a word. He couldn't speak. He was a skeleton reaching out to touch me. He clutched my hand and looked at me for over five minutes, his sunken eyes saying, "make sure to take care of Sara, while I'm gone."

And, on the fifth day, we got the call. Sid had passed that morning.

Jeremy and Lisa had already returned to San Diego barely two weeks before. They now had to fly back again for his funeral.

As difficult as Sid was, as much as he was in denial about his own aging and mortality, as difficult as it was to get him to sign his will, amazingly, somewhere along the line he agreed to let us pre-plan his funeral. The funeral went according to plan without a single hiccup. It didn't make the emotions less raw, but it was one less thing to worry about during a difficult time.

We're going to talk next about how and why to pre-plan a funeral and why, you should plan yours at the same time.

Eternity Planning

There is a common misconception that funerals are for the dead. They're really for the living. They're meant to be a celebration of the departed person's life, not their death.

We don't attend our own funerals. Our family and friends do. They remember how we lived, how we touched their lives when we were alive and how we still touch their lives after we passed.

When an elderly family member passes, especially after suffering from an illness, we may feel a sense of relief. Finally, their suffering has ended. They're no longer in pain.

Then we feel guilty about feeling relieved, as if we're secretly glad they're gone. But it's not joy we feel. It's still grief just masquerading as relief.

Sara and I have participated in seven funerals, four of which, for our parents, we've had to arrange completely on our own.

And the grief doesn't get easier each time. The next time isn't any better than the last time. It's not something that gets better with practice. It's an emptiness you feel inside whenever any family member passes.

For my father Norman, the first parent to pass, my mother Phyllis was incapable of handling the arrangements. She had to be brought to the funeral home and arrived with her walker and then sat quietly in the funeral director's office, while Sara and I arranged everything.

The same for Sara's mother Eleanor, who died three weeks to the day after my dad. Sidney was in a state of total shock during the whole ordeal and sat listless in the funeral director's office, while we handled everything. He couldn't believe his wife of over 60 years was now gone.

Unfortunately, we've been a customer so many times at our neighborhood funeral home, we're a celebrity there. We're on a first name basis with the funeral directors.

Our experience has taught us, just as with everything else related to elder care, to plan as far ahead as possible. Even while planning mom and dad's future funeral, you should be planning your own, and your spouse's, as well, even if you're young.

A pre-planned funeral will not only take away the burden of making funeral arrangements when you're in your worst possible emotional state and not thinking clearly, it will also lessen the financial burden by locking in the costs ahead of time. There won't be any surprise charges, which you're not mentally prepared to deal with while mourning your loved one.

If you're parent is in a nursing home, they will ask for the name of the funeral home to contact in case of death. It will be on one of the forms in the hundred-page-plus package of registration documents.

There is nothing more stressful than sitting in a funeral director's office, sometimes for hours, arranging a funeral at the last minute, right after someone dies, when everything could have been handled ahead of time. Instead of hours, the meeting with the funeral director will be brief, maybe less than an hour, to schedule the ceremony and burial and go over minor details. The rest of the details are in the pre-planning documents.

This is the morbid part of elder care, the part nobody wants to talk about, the part everybody hates to deal with. But the further ahead you plan, the less stressful it becomes. Sara and I have gone through this enough that sadly, it has become routine. It still doesn't take away the pain of mourning, but it's one less thing to think about when mom or dad has passed away.

Funeral People Aren't Creepy

Our experience has been that funeral people aren't morose or creepy. They're pretty much like everybody else. They aren't draped in Dracula capes with top hats over widow's peaks and with ghoulish grins exposing pointy fangs, and funeral homes aren't dark dungeons with creaky doors covered in cobwebs and bats screeching overhead.

But the industry has consolidated and become corporate and sometimes impersonal. The old neighborhood funeral home, which used to be owned and operated by a local family everybody in town knew, may still have the family's name on the door, but may now be part of a chain owned by a corporation. Some have become integrated businesses owning groups of funeral homes and cemeteries around the country.

We have found the funeral business to be notorious for its euphemisms. A pre-planned funeral, rather than being called "pre-planned" is called a "pre-need." The fee for digging a grave and covering it up after burial is called an "opening and closing charge."

Planning a Funeral in Advance

Don't let the industry jargon dissuade you from pre-planning a funeral. You just need to be aware of all the charges to make sure you buy only the services you need and not unnecessary extras. The following are some tips from our experience.

Whether you're just doing a simple cremation or a full service with a wake before the funeral or a shiva or other visitation after the funeral, there are several options.

A lot of what you choose will depend on both your personal preferences, your religion and, of course, your pocketbook.

Whatever you do, it can all be part of the "pre-need" instructions.

Different Types of Arrangements

The cheapest option is to just cremate your deceased family member. This has become popular not just because of the cost, but also because it's the most environmentally friendly, if that was important to the deceased, and because it's quick and easy. Some religions, like Judaism, prohibit cremation but even a Jewish funeral home may still do it at the family's request.

The urn with the deceased's ashes can either be given to the family or put in a mausoleum at the cemetery. Each urn is put in its own vault marked with an engraving or a plaque resembling a headstone. Vaults can either be for individuals or for families who want their urns together.

A ceremony, sometimes called a Celebration of Life, for family and friends can then be held another day somewhere other than a funeral home or place of worship. We've seen families have them catered in a party room at a restaurant.

These types of ceremonies, a sort of funeral without the deceased, where the burial is done separately, have also become popular. They may also be held sometime after a private burial, where the family holds a service at the gravesite only for family members.

Another option is having the service at the gravesite, skipping the funeral home or house of worship altogether. This has become popular because it's cheaper and easier. The whole service is done at the cemetery without a car procession through busy streets and traffic.

During the Covid pandemic and the shutdown, funerals went online. Since then, some funeral homes now offer services via Zoom, both at the funeral home or house of worship and at the graveside. This may be appropriate for out-of-town family and friends who can't attend in person. Sara and I once attended a Zoom funeral in Milwaukee from the comfort of our dining room at our home in suburban Chicago.

When my mother Phyllis died of Covid, right at the height of an early wave of the pandemic, I didn't have a funeral, just a simple burial. The only people in attendance, besides myself, were someone from the funeral home and a close friend. I was the rabbi, saying the mourner's kaddish, and a few prayers and Psalms.

Make sure the funeral director itemizes everything offered in the pre-need before signing the contract. Items might include the casket and concrete vault, handling of the deceased's body and burial preparation, the hearse, and the use of the funeral home's sanctuary and facilities. Packages differ, so make sure to spell out exactly what you need.

The package might not include the cost of the burial – the so-called "opening and closing charge" – or the cemetery plots, often purchased separately directly from the cemetery, the fee for the obituary – charged by the newspaper not the funeral home – and the cost of a member of the clergy to officiate. You can also design and prepay for the headstones with the cemetery, so that when the time comes only the date of death has to be engraved on the stone.

There may be an additional charge for visitations, such as a wake at the funeral home, or a shiva, the Jewish visitation after the ceremony, if catered at the funeral home. Jewish custom is to have the shiva at the family's home, but the funeral home may offer catering packages at an additional charge.

The funeral home offers other helpful services to be aware of.

They can assist in finding a clergy member, if you don't have a favorite priest, minister, rabbi or imam, for example. If you don't know a member of the clergy, one can be assigned to you. That person will want to sit down with the family before the ceremony and gather information about the deceased to put their eulogy together.

The clergy member will also want to go over the details of the ceremony. If anybody wants to give a eulogy, this is the time to make sure it's added to the schedule.

Not Just Funerals: Other Services Offered

The funeral home will notify Social Security on your behalf to end benefits, one less thing for you to think about, or forget. They will provide some death certificates, essential for settling the estate, at no cost. If you need more, they have to be purchased from your local department of vital records.

The funeral home will also write the cookie-cutter obituary for the newspaper based on the information about the family you give them. The wording of obituaries is canned and follows a similar template. If you want an additional, more detailed, obituary, if your family member was famous or well-known, contact news outlets directly.

The funeral home may also offer discounts with some airlines on travel for out-of-town family members wanting to attend the ceremony. If the deceased family member has to be transported back home, depending on the airline, a family member may be able to fly free of charge on the same plane. The funeral home arranges transportation and pickup at the airport of the deceased and will have information about arrival times and procedures.

So, you've decided to take the plunge and get a pre-need. Now, how do you pay for it?

A pre-need is actually a scaled-down term life insurance policy. Sometimes, it's advertised as burial insurance, though unlike a pre-need, it may only cover the cost of burial and not a funeral. It can be paid upfront in full, which is like paying for the full funeral in advance or, like an insurance policy, in monthly installments.

This is another reason to get a pre-need. Since it's an insurance policy, it can be transferred to another funeral home in case your funeral home goes out of business.

Whether it's paid up front or in installments, a life insurance company will send you an annual statement on the status of the account. The funeral home contracts with the life insurance company in case the funeral home goes out of business before the policy holder passes, and you need to move the funeral to another home.

The moment your family member passes, whether at home by your side, or when you get a phone call from the nursing home, call the funeral home immediately to pick up the deceased, even if in the middle of the night or on a weekend or holiday. The funeral home has someone on call around the clock every day of the year to arrange pickup and delivery to their facility.

The nursing home may make that call for you first, but it's still a good idea for you to contact the funeral home directly yourself to check your deceased loved one is being picked up.

If you're not sure someone at home has passed – it's not always easy to tell if someone has stopped breathing or is just in a deep sleep – call 911. They will confirm if someone is deceased, and then you can call the funeral home. The police may show up first, which routinely happens, to confirm there was no foul play and to "clear the scene" first before you can arrange transport to the funeral home.

Sara and I have gotten that phone call from either the hospice, hospital, or nursing home for all four of our parents before having had to turn around and immediately make that unpleasant call to the funeral home ourselves.

None of our parents died at home, and we never went through the agony of seeing them being zipped up in a body bag and taken away by the funeral home. We've heard how unpleasant it is from those that have gone through it.

I know this whole discussion has been depressing. Just think of pre-planning as one of those chores we all have to do. Then put it in a drawer and forget about it, until you need it. In the meantime, be obsessed with living your life.

Eternity Planning

- Decide on burial or cremation
- Decide which type of service
  - ➢ Traditional
  - ➢ Graveside
  - ➢ Celebration of Life later
- Purchase a Pre-Need
  - ➢ Purchase cemetery plot
  - ➢ Design and pay for headstone
- Call funeral home at time of passing
- Funeral home services
  - ➢ Obituary
  - ➢ Finding clergy to officiate
  - ➢ Death certificates

Dementia Diaries

Dementia is no laughing matter, but we've heard people with dementia say some funny things. Watching your family members age is no fun, but listening to some of the silly things they say sometimes can provide a little bit of comic relief from an otherwise tragic situation.

First, we need to explain exactly what dementia is, and isn't. People throw around the word dementia anytime an old person forgets even one small thing.

Dementia isn't just forgetting, something we all do at any age. Whenever someone elderly forgets anything, we're quick to diagnosis it unprofessionally as dementia.

This isn't the case.

Dementia is a pattern of cognitive decline, beyond just forgetting where you put your keys. It's not just isolated incidents of misplacing things around the house, which we've all done, or forgetting where you're going. It's a continuous pattern of confusion and misjudgment, loss of judgment and thinking that disrupt daily life.

Doctors can test for it by asking simple questions about daily life and current events that anyone should be able to answer easily, such as who is the president, what day it is, or what city they're in.

Someone with dementia would answer with a straight face with a day, month or even year other than today, a president from their youth decades ago, or some distant town they might have visited in the past. They say it with such conviction, it's almost believable, at least from their facial expressions and body language.

Dementia is the mental side of aging, coinciding with physical decline. They may occur at the same time, or not in synch, at all. There are elderly people who decline physically but don't lose it mentally until the very end. Then there are others who decline mentally but not physically until, of course, when they just suddenly expire and pass.

"We're All Doomed"

When I asked a neurologist once at a social event, if there was any way to prevent dementia, he answered, "We're all doomed." He later clarified that it's inevitable, just like physical decline, if we live long enough. No one is spared.

Dementia is the umbrella term for all age-related mental decline. Alzheimer's is only one of those ailments. Again, too often, people throw around the word Alzheimer's for anyone with dementia.

172

Symptoms of Alzheimer's resemble dementia – memory loss, confusion, cognitive decline, and personality changes and mood swings – but Alzheimer's is caused by physical changes in the brain.

They look alike, but can only be diagnosed by a medical professional. Don't try and guess yourself. Take mom or dad to a doctor.

There are no known cures, but there is medication that can ease some of the symptoms, such as belligerent behavior. Doctors had to prescribe medication for both Phyllis and Sid to calm them down and stop combative behavior towards us and staff at their nursing homes.

Never, never try to reason with someone with dementia. It will go nowhere and can frustrate, even anger, your elderly family member. Just play along and say yes. What you, or they say, doesn't matter anymore. It's all just talk now.

There was the divorced guy who forgot he was divorced. He had stayed friendly with his ex-wife all his life. When his ex-wife told him they were divorced, he said, "Well, then, we should get married again!"

There was the World War II veteran who had fought in Italy and told his family he was still waiting for his orders for deployment and, meanwhile, covered the windows with towels to block snipers outside, just in case.

There was Sid's cousin – before Sid had dementia himself – who had dementia and called him every two weeks to tell him her husband had died. She forgot every time she called that she had already called two weeks before. This went on for a few months, until she finally figured it out.

There was Phyllis wondering why Norman wasn't visiting her in the nursing home. I had to tell her he had died eight years before. She bowed her head and cried. It was heartbreaking.

Then there was Sid himself, whose dementia seemed to get worse at night. For a while, he was only fine during the day. We called him a "sundowner" because he seemed to get worse at night.

He went from calling us to get him out of the nursing home, because "They're trying to kill me," to calling us during a shift change to say, "The rats are leaving the sinking ship." There was the story about the shopping center he never visited in Moscow based on a real trip he took to the Ukraine with his mother decades before during the Cold War. They had only visited Kiev, where his mother was born, not Moscow.

Then there was Norman who told the doctors in the emergency room, when asked who was the president, that he only knew he had a Black wife. He had forgotten Obama's name. When asked where they were – Chicago – Norman said Cleveland, where a heart institute he had considered for treatment, was located.

The funniest were Grandma Ida's antics in the nursing home.

She asked me why my brother didn't come to visit. I'm an only child. I told her he was busy. She asked how the restaurant business was doing. I've never owned a restaurant in my life. I said it was doing well. She told me she was getting on the train the next day to see out-of-town family. I wished her a good trip.

She asked us for cash, so she could tip the waiters. She told us, at age 98, she needed a man. She had already outlived three husbands. I guess she was looking to break a record with a fourth one.

One day she stood in front of the cafeteria in the nursing home and thanked everyone for attending the wedding, probably reliving the many, many family weddings she had attended during her hundred-year lifetime.

Maybe it was better she didn't know where she was. At least, she still had the spirit to be happy, even in a nursing home.

Paying for Elder Care

The cost of elder care can be astronomical. Even if you're willing and able to take care of mom and dad at home, you still need to retrofit the house for elder accessibility – guardrails, raised toilet seats, handrails in bathrooms and showers and, if there are stairs inside and outside the house, stairlifts inside and a ramp outside.

All these additions cost money. So, even if the idea is to avoid the cost of caregivers and assisted living or nursing homes, think again. Getting old isn't cheap.

Then, on top of the cost to make the house accessible, there are seemingly endless medical bills for doctors and medication, not to mention equipment like walkers and wheelchairs or oxygen tanks.

Start With Medicare

The first place to start is with Medicare. If a doctor can prescribe something, check if it might be covered by Medicare. For example, it could cost thousands of dollars to install stairlifts out of pocket. If prescribed by a doctor, Medicare might cover most or all the cost. But Medicare rules are constantly changing, so check first before claiming any benefits, especially if not related directly to medical care, like stairlifts.

Medicare can be taken starting at age 65. The details of Medicare programs are beyond the scope of this book. Plans and programs vary greatly depending on where someone lives. Consult a Medicare professional to pick the best plan for you and your elderly family members.

Medicare has four parts:

- Part A – Hospital visits
- Part B – Outpatient care, like doctor visits
- Part C – Parts A, B and D bundled together
          Also called Medicare Advantage
- Part D – Prescription drugs

. . . and two payment plans:

- Medicare Advantage
- Medicare Supplemental

Part A is covered by the federal government for both Advantage and Supplemental plans. You don't have to pay anything out of pocket.

Medicare Advantage, called Part C, is a single payer plan combining the other three Parts (A, B and D) into a single part paid by a private insurance company approved by Medicare. Instead of paying

Medicare directly, you make a single payment each month to the insurance company.

Prescription drug coverage can be through either an Advantage plan that includes Part D or paid separately through another insurance company. If you pay Part D separately, it won't be included in your Advantage plan.

In a Supplemental plan, you pay Medicare directly for Part B and then pay for Part D for prescription drugs through a Medicare-approved insurer.

If you're already getting Social Security, Part B is automatically deducted from your monthly benefit. If you're not yet taking Social Security, you have to pay Part B on your own out of pocket.

Advantage plans may also include dental and eye care and other perks, such as health club membership, sometimes affectionately called Silver Sneakers.

Supplemental plans don't include dental and eye care, which must be purchased separately. You're also on your own for health club membership.

Advantage versus Supplemental

Supplemental plans are more expensive than Advantage plans but provide better coverage. You also have only one bill with Advantage but have separate bills under Supplemental for Part B and the additional services you purchase, like dental and eye care, for example.

The catch with the convenience of Advantage plans is that not every doctor or medical service is in their network. Supplemental plans offer broader coverage. You don't want to be surprised at the doctor that your visit or procedure isn't covered.

Again, as with everything discussed here, check your Medicare providers for the most accurate and up-to-date information and to see which plan, Advantage or Supplemental, is better for your family.

Often the route to a nursing home starts with mom or dad in an emergency room followed by a brief stint in the hospital, then a longer stay in rehab at a nursing home, where they may end up staying for long-term care.

Medicare may cover up to 90 days of rehab at a nursing home. The hospital usually picks the rehab facility and arranges moving mom or dad there. They will pick what is convenient for them, not you, and it may not be a nice place. If you want your elderly family member moved to another facility, other than the one the hospital picks, because it's closer or nicer, you need to tell the hospital before they're released.

When your elderly family member finally arrives at the nursing home, Medicare may also cover some additional physical therapy for a limited time. At some point, Medicare stops covering physical therapy from an outside professional beyond what the nursing staff already provides.

Sidney kept asking for physical therapy long after his coverage had expired. He thought if the therapy continued, he would be able to walk again and drive home and go back to work. Despite nagging her endlessly, Sara finally had to just tell him it wasn't covered any more.

Not every elderly person in rehab ends up in a nursing home, like Sid. Medicare covered two 90-day stints each in rehab for Phyllis, one for a fall and another after a serious illness. She returned home after both stays. Her route to the nursing home, as previously discussed, wasn't via rehab.

Competition for Medicare Advantage plans is fierce. The open enrollment period is from October to December. During that time, your mailbox, both your physical one and your virtual one – in your e-mail and on your cellphone – will be full with calls from insurance salespeople hawking their shiny new plans.

Next is Social Security

If your elderly parents have already started taking Social Security, the Part B premium is automatically deducted each month from their Social Security check.

Assuming your elderly parents are already over 65, they can start collecting their full Social Security benefit at age 67, if they were born after 1960. Those born before 1960, which includes the bulk of Boomers, can start taking Social Security at 66.

Ideally, if their finances can hold out, they should try to wait until age 70, when they're entitled to the maximum benefit. Unfortunately, many people get kicked out of the job market through layoffs or illness long before then, some as early as 62, the earliest age when benefits can be collected.

If that happens, they may feel like they're being penalized twice, first, for being forced to look for a job, even if they're able and willing, in an unforgiving and competitive job market not open to hiring people over age 60 and, second, by not being able to ever recover their full Social Security benefits.

If you take Social Security at 62, you get the lowest possible benefit and your benefits stay at that level for the rest of your life. You can't reapply to claim a higher rate later when you reach 67 or 70, the age when you would have normally filed for benefits.

Besides Social Security, there are other ways to pay for elder care.

Let's start with the worst scenario. Mom and dad are completely destitute and have no savings or money, at all. In that case, Medicaid can pay for a nursing home. But your choices are limited. They pick the nursing home, based on what they can pay, which may not be the closest or nicest facility.

The next step up is relying on a combination of monthly Social Security benefits and income from a pension plan. The nursing home may want your family member's Social Security check assigned directly to the home. This might sound, at first, like a great idea – one less bill to pay each month – but be careful. There could be a lot of paperwork and headaches, if you decide to cancel the direct assignment later, or want to change nursing homes.

Nursing homes may also ask other intimate questions about your finances to prove your ability to make monthly payments. They may ask for lists of assets and bank accounts. You have to decide what information you feel comfortable providing.

We ran into a few nursing homes that asked for more details than necessary about our finances. They should only need information to meet state and federal regulations and to determine if you might eventually need Medicaid. Otherwise, stay away from nursing homes, as we did, that ask too much.

Pension income? Who gets pensions anymore? Remember your elderly family member may have started work in ancient times, before IRAs and 401Ks even existed, when companies routinely provided pensions.

Though corporate pensions are rare, or nonexistent, today people who retire from the military, government, or other public service, such as the police, may still get some sort of pension. Other professions may offer savings and investment programs, such as Teachers Insurance and Annuity Association of America (TIAA) for teachers and professors, which are similar to pensions.

After Social Security and pensions, there are IRAs and 401Ks that may have been offered through your elderly family member's employer. Then, of course, mom and dad might have had savings in a bank or investment accounts at a brokerage firm, where they put money for their retirement.

The same companies offering IRAs and 401Ks through employers, such as Vanguard, Schwab or Fidelity, to name just a few, also offer brokerage and investment accounts for individuals. These companies also have representatives to help tailor a plan based on your income, age and need.

Paying for your parent's elder care aside, you're never too young yourself to start saving for retirement and should take advantage of any savings or IRA and 401K plan offered by your company. If not provided by your employer, you're on your own and should still try to set aside savings for your own elder care through the investment companies just mentioned.

The last source of income for elder care is your parent's home. If they no longer live there, and you're not planning to take it over when they pass away, and if they've paid off the mortgage, the proceeds from the sale can also help cover the costs of assisted living and nursing homes.

Other Sources: Private Payers and Medicaid

If you're writing a single check yourself each month to the nursing home from all the above sources, you're what they call a "private payer." Nursing homes love private payers.

A nursing home owner once told me a horror story about going to a meeting with a government agency in a room filled with other frustrated nursing home owners waiting for months to get paid. With a private payer, at least, they don't have to wait for their money. As a private payer, you're also more likely to get better service.

We've found nursing homes will do whatever it takes to keep their private payers from leaving.

So, what happens, even after scrimping and saving all their life, the money well runs dry? There's still always Medicaid.

It's still always best, no matter your income, to talk to a financial professional, whether your local banker or an investment advisor, and plan as soon as possible for the inevitable.

Heaven isn't on schedule and doesn't take credit cards.

Paying for Elder Care

- Savings
- Pensions
- Social Security
- Life insurance
- Medicare
- IRA/401K
- Assets
  - Investment/brokerage accounts
  - Real Estate/sale of home
- Medicaid

Elder Care Checklist

Sara and I don't have children. We have nieces and children of other family members to whom we've given instructions for our care in old age.

We've set up powers of attorney, for both property and healthcare, living wills and trusts, and then wills with executors and successor executors. We have complete lists of all our banking and investment accounts and added other family members as joint owners.

Then, of course, we've purchased pre-needs and cemetery plots for ourselves.

The following is a summary of everything covered in this book that can serve as a checklist for both caring for your elderly parents and preparing an elder care plan for yourselves:

Legal Documents
1. Powers of attorney (POA)
    a. Property
    b. Health Care
        i. Living Will
        ii. Do Not Resuscitate (DNR)
2. Contact information for estate attorney
3. Will and trust documents
    a. Name of executor and successors

4. Location of the following documents
    a. List of all assets
    b. Set up joint ownership and beneficiaries
    c. Checking, savings, bank accounts
    d. Investment accounts
    e. IRAs and 401Ks
    f. Pensions
    g. Real estate
    h. Life insurance policies
    i. Social Security card
5. Death certificate

Living Arrangements
1. Home care or outside facility
2. If home care, DIY or a caregiver
    a. Retrofit the house
        i. Guardrails
        ii. Stairlifts
3. If hire a caregiver, independent or through an agency
    a. Check agency
    b. Registered with the state
    c. Complaints with the state
    d. Bonded and insured
    e. References for caregivers
    f. Cost of caregiver
    g. Remove from home
        i. Valuables
        ii. Financial documents
4. Assisted living or nursing home

a. Walk through facility
    i. Meet management and staff
    ii. Check if facility is clean
    iii. Check if there is enough staff
    iv. Location of nursing stations
    v. Staff/resident atmosphere
    vi. Check the rooms
    vii. Guardrails: bed and bath
b. Agree on price and payment plan
    i. Complete paperwork
    ii. Get medical records
c. Contact numbers at nursing home

Eternity Planning
1. Purchase a pre-need plan based on
    a. Whether burial or cremation
    b. Type of service and visitation
        i. Traditional
        ii. Gravesite
        iii. Celebration of Life
2. Buy cemetery plots
    a. Prepay burial charges
    b. Design and pay for headstone

Paying for Elder Care
1. Savings
2. Pensions
3. Social Security
4. Life insurance
5. Medicare
    a. Supplemental or Advantage

6. IRA/401K
7. Assets
   a. Investments
   b. Stocks/Bonds
   c. Real Estate
8. Sale of home
9. Medicaid

www.ingramcontent.com/pod-product-compliance
Lightning Source LLC
Chambersburg PA
CBHW060420130626
46555CB00005B/2139